TH
COOL SIDE
OF MY
PILLOW

THE COOL SIDE OF MY PILLOW

A BOOK OF ESSAYS BY

BRUCE CAMPBELL

CONTENTS

It would be shortsighted to put out a book of essays without addressing our current challenge – this COVID-19 business. When this all started going down in March 2020, my first reaction was, *holy shit, this could be a game-changer*, much the way I felt in 2001, seeing images of the planes hitting the Twin Towers in New York City. 9/11 sent out a worldwide shockwave and pitted civilizations against each other, perhaps permanently. I'm not a doom-and-gloom guy – at least not out loud – but I have the core feeling that this virus will leave its mark on every inhabitant – physically, mentally or economically, like a worldwide 9/11.

When lockdowns started mid-March, I was grateful to have the luck of timing – 2020 was to be a year of writing and pitching new projects, so travel wasn't in the cards anyway and professional obligations were kept to a minimum.

Then, with LOTS of extra time to think, it dawned on me just how my own world was likely to change.

Over the last three years, I travelled to ninety-nine cities, averaging thirty-three a year, or basically hauling my ass to a new city every week and a half. In the future, how is that supposed to work? The travel consequences alone stagger me. I flew enough that TSA agents, while still doing their duties, would give me a familiar nod or a "Where you off to this week?" I'm sure they got very familiar with my black Briggs & Riley backpack, carrying the exact same things each time: two empty thermoses (a red one for coffee, a blue one for water), my iPad, a myriad of chargers, noise-cancelling headphones, vape pen, wintergreen chewing gum, cash and wallet. None of it was exciting or dangerous, but that was my life – connecting from Medford, Oregon, usually through Denver, Phoenix or Salt Lake to destinations beyond.

Ironically, after years of despising travel, I had begun to enjoy it again. As much as anyone could, I thought I finally got travel "down." I knew how to book flights with great connections, how to pack, *what* to pack (including hotel room hacks), what seats on a plane I liked – which airlines and hotels were great and which ones sucked. I paid attention to the square footage of a hotel room when booking and I cared about what floor I was on and whether the hotel had room service, so I could predict my eating schedule when time was tight.

Apps really helped play the game, so I had every airline, hotel and transportation app and used them almost daily.

2

As long as you didn't need to deal with an actual human, you could get around this country pretty easily without even a phone call.

With the future of travel, I'm not waiting for the other *shoe* to drop as much as I'm waiting for entire *hubs* to drop. It took twenty years to get most of the major airlines into my humble airport. I wonder what will be left of our airline industry when this shakes out. Medford International Airport didn't have the greatest connections in the *best* of times. Aircraft pulling in and out of MFR were generally "not new" and "not big." Interestingly, our airport can handle huge cargo tankers because of forest fires, so we have the tarmac – we just don't have the population to support big planes, because we couldn't fill them.

"I said 'six feet', mother-scratcher!"

There comes a point when it isn't about the virus anymore – because a vaccine will surely come – it's about what will be left when the economic dust settles. Every business has contacts, clients and suppliers. Even as a "two-person band" with my wife Ida, our Campbell Entertainment did pump a certain amount of cash into local, national and international economies.

Locally, my dry cleaners will take a hit just from my absence. When I was at my touring peak a couple years ago, the amount of stuff I dropped off every other week would throw your back out. They were always delighted to see me. They must think I got hit by a bus.

I fear for my local economy as a whole. The biggest city in our area is Medford. Known also as "Methford," it has its share of disenfranchised people. On a bike ride along our greenway, the amount and general disposition of these folks has increased and declined, all at the same time. The local paper writes about the emergence of a more "aggressive" homeless population. A number of service agencies had to close because of social distancing, so more folks already on the edge are being forced into the bushes, literally. Desperation and despair can make decent folks tilt in the wrong direction.

I have a sense that numerous local bars and restaurants are not going to come out the other side. Maybe some of the institutional places will survive just by sheer will, but I feel for the entrepreneur who had *just* opened or invested in a restaurant. Even those that do survive – as well as venues like movie theaters – the question remains: even if you open, will people show up, or will they be too afraid or too tapped out financially?

Lots of questions remain.

A personal observation is that I have never washed

more dishes in my life. I'm not complaining, because I'm eating three fabulous, home-cooked meals a day, but every time I'd turn around there was a new pile of dishes – and we're only two people. Why does it seem like I'm doing so many more damn dishes? After two months of prune-y fingers, it dawned on me: I used to eat out a LOT. In a given week, I would surely eat at least one meal a day away from home.

One of my favorite pastimes, which has a murky post-virus future, is pulling up a stool at a local bar and killing some time with pals. If the "new normal" is dudes sitting by themselves, six feet apart, it might not look good on a bar's Facebook page.

Or maybe it does! Maybe we have gotten tired of being elbowed on airplanes and herded into restaurants. I'm very happy to not have some A-type traveler up my ass when I'm boarding a plane. In a crowded world, maybe we all could use a little extra personal space.

Honestly, I long for the first opportunity to return to my local Elks Lodge and shoot the shit. I don't expect the experience to be the same, or even feel the same, but I'm hoping for a return to "sort of normal."

Professionally, I thought I was on easy street. I spent forty years in the film business and it felt right to scale back to enjoy ugly golf and beautiful granddaughters. I had the perfect master plan: take road trips with my wife Ida, ride bikes, swim, hike, smoke reefer, go to a horror, sci-fi or fantasy convention once a month, wear goofy outfits, drink tequila martinis and BS with fans. The idea was to do this until I dropped dead at the ripe old age of 96 during a layover in Detroit – fittingly, in an airport terminal. Boy, did I get the last thirty years of my life wrong!

Aside from packing humans into planes like sardines, a typical day at a convention also represented a lot of close quarters, human interaction. Right off the bat, I'd always start with photo ops because my hair was in place and my gaudy outfit didn't have any wrinkles yet.

Four poses you might never see again...

I make it a point of shaking the hand of everyone who walks through for a photo op – old and young. I was never sure if I would see them later for autographs, so I wanted to make sure they at least had "a moment." I also wasn't concerned about hygiene. I'm a clean guy, but I'm not a "germophobe." I'm actually one of these weirdos who think hand sanitizer is the enemy and that humans need to build their immune systems through interaction with other humans. I washed my hands plenty of times at cons but never enough to suit my nervous agent, Mike

Estes, who was driven crazy by my lack of attention to the whole thing.

Proximity at cons is a big deal for fans. They pay good money to see their favorite personality "up close and personal." Fans love making up poses for actors during these photo sessions, and many of them involve physical contact. Numerous women have wanted me to "dip" them romantically or clutch my leg, mirroring the poster from *Army of Darkness*.

Looking back at decades of convention photos, you'd be hard pressed to find one where I didn't have a hand on someone's shoulder, or giving them rabbit ears, or posing with three dudes like a record album cover. No matter what the pose, we were always right on top of each other. I felt sorry for the *Walking Dead* dudes, because their female fans were relentlessly "grabby." Okay, I didn't really feel sorry for them, but that "closeness" would never pass muster now.

The convention scene is going to have a challenging time getting back up to speed. I was supposed to do promotion at the 2020 Electronics Expo, The New York Comic-Con and the mother of all Cons in San Diego – all now cancelled. When they begin to book conventions again, what will a post-viral "photo op" look like? I picture a backdrop now twelve, or eighteen feet wide in order to accommodate me in the middle and one person on each side, six feet away. And, are we wearing masks? For a photo? If I have to wear a mask at these events and you can't see my face, why the hell would I even go?

Believe me, I hope we can figure this out before we all light our hair on fire. I had also just finished a tour of "An Evening With..." type appearances where I would show up at cool old movie theaters, show a beloved old movie, crack jokes and get the hell out of there. This was the type of appearance I was hoping to increase in number. Now, like every other person on the planet, I don't really know when that will resume.

I have a couple movie opportunities in the near future and I'm really curious how that will change. Now, when actors have an "intimate" scene, will they present documentation as proof of being "free from infectious diseases?" Movie sets are sweaty mosh pits of sustained activity. Very often, crew members work shoulder-to-shoulder in order to fulfill their on-set duties. I am more than a little curious to see how my industry will adapt.

On a personal note, aside from markedly increased levels of unprovoked irritability, I guess I could say I'm doing okay. In the early weeks of self-isolation, I watched a lot of news. It's a natural reaction when potentially life-altering things are happening, but it soon became to be too much for my psyche, let alone my eyes. I had to dial it back. I now check headlines on Mondays, and that has worked really well. Now, I only get pissed off and freaked out once a week instead of every day.

Am I worried about the future? Hell yes. You'd have to be brain dead not to be. I've never faced this level of uncertainty in my life. The rhythms we took for granted are changing fast – hell, even the seasons are not the same anymore. For me, the most unsettling aspect of this current situation is the loss of predictability.

In super-weird times like these, people will be tested. Some will rise and others will fall spectacularly. Personally, I feel that the key to life is being able to adapt. Jobs my grandfather had at Alcoa Aluminum for forty-four years just don't exist anymore. I'm grateful for the modular life the entertainment business has provided – I'm used to long periods with no income and I can ply my trade almost anywhere in the world.

As a result of COVID-19, people will be forced to change their habitual routine – and we might have to face a future that doesn't have a rosy, Hollywood ending. I am resolved to get through this with as much dignity as I can and help others whenever possible. Hopefully, the takeaway of this pandemic will be people treating each other a little better. I would be very okay with that.

HAIL TO THE KING

It's no secret that author Stephen King helped put *Evil Dead* on the map. In the Spring of 1983 at the Cannes Film Festival, Mr. King attended a screening of our little movie, which was there being sold internationally.

His reaction, when we found out about it, made our hair stand on end. Apparently, after Cannes, Stephen King penned a story for *Twilight Zone* magazine about *Evil Dead*. The words "most ferociously original horror film of the year" jumped off the page, because reviews and reactions to the film weren't great up to that point – an Atlanta paper called *Evil Dead* "the sickest of the sick." *The Christian Science Monitor* called it "a film that stooped."

On top of that, we couldn't find a US distributor – it's why we started selling the film overseas. As filmmakers in the throes of selling their first movie, we simply had to have that quote. I don't even know how we tracked a guy like Stephen King down in those days, but the request went in. Again, his **yes** reply gave us a happy whiplash. We could use the quote, we just had to tweak it to say "...of 1983" instead of "...of the year." It couldn't imply that *Evil Dead* was the most "ferociously original horror film *forever*." It made sense, and we gleefully slapped it on the top of the poster.

'THE EVIL DEAD'
Why you haven't seen it yet . . .
and why you ought to
by Stephen King

WHILE ON THE SCENE AT CANNES, THE AUTHOR STUMBLED UPON—WELL, NOT GOLD, EXACTLY, BUT PLENTY OF GREAT GORE.

In Sam Raimi's still-unreleased *The Evil Dead*, the stalwart hero, played by Bruce Campbell (left), is forced to contend with some highly ambulatory corpses (right) ...

... and discovers that solid walls offer surprisingly little protection.

When I met Sam Raimi at the Cannes Film Festival in May of 1982, my first thought was that this fellow was one of three things: a busboy, a runaway American high school student, or a genius. He wasn't a busboy, and Raimi finished high school some time ago, although he has the sort of ageless sophomore looks that are going to keep bartenders asking to see his driver's license or state liquor card until he's at least thirty-five. That he is a genius is yet unproven; that he has made the most ferociously original horror film of 1982 seems to me beyond doubt. The only problem is that you may never see it.

Farnsworth Wright, the legendary editor of *Weird Tales* in the 1930s, admitted—with some reluctance—that he had rejected one story, *one single story*, on the grounds that it might well be too gruesome for current tastes. The tale, by William Hope Hodgson, had to do with a maniac who was killing people and turning them into soup (this same idea formed the basis for Stanley Ellin's classic debut story, "The Specialty of the House," some fifteen years later). "When it's too much," Wright said, "class doesn't matter."

This may be the case with Raimi's film *The Evil Dead*. Take a good look at the accompanying stills, dear reader, because most of the large American film distribution nets have now passed on Raimi's independently financed film. (The

latest to pass was Paramount, which distributed the hugely successful—if brainless—*Friday the 13th*, their verdict, like Wright's, was that too much was just too much.)

Raimi, a Michigan native now quartered near Detroit, was twenty when he directed and wrote *Evil Dead*. (He was also one of the cameramen, assisted in the first half by Tim Philo.) His producer, Rob Tapert, was twenty-six. The gruesome special effects were achieved in tandem by Tom Sullivan, twenty-four, and Bart Pierce, who is ... The five st... .....

college kids. The film was shot in sixteen millimeter and blown up to thirty-five for theatrical release. The resulting effect is grainy but oddly apt; the film has a weirdly convincing documentary look that no one has seen since George Romero's *Night of the Living Dead*, a film Raimi admits was a strong influence.

The Evil Dead has the simple, stupid power of a good campfire story—but its simplicity is not a side effect. It is something carefully crafted by Raimi, who is anything ...

Stephen King roared back to prominence with *It* and remains a towering figure in the literary world, but in 1983 he was **STEPHEN KING!** His endorsement sent a shockwave through the world of movie critics that effectively protected us from getting panned. Not long after his endorsement, a review came in from the *Los Angeles Times*. Among other things, critic Kevin Thomas called *Evil Dead* "an instant classic." Wow. That was a fast turnaround! Mind you, this was the same movie. We hadn't touched a frame. As they say in Hollywood, "perception" is 9/10 the law. In this case, Stephen King says the movie is good – so the movie is good!

Upstart distribution company New Line Cinema took notice and agreed to market the film domestically, and we were off to the races. They advanced us a fee for the rights, but never anything beyond that. It was our introduction to "Hollywood bookkeeping" – meaning, they "keep" the books. Mercifully, *Evil Dead* was a hit in Europe. In some markets, we were second only to *E.T.*

Home entertainment is what finally put the movie into profit. *Evil Dead* arrived when VHS tape rentals were exploding, and it wasn't long before a million "units" were sold – which at the time put us right up there with *Lady and the Tramp*, so our investors were very happy.

With a first "home run" under our belt, Sam Raimi, Rob Tapert and I set out to make a "Hollywood" movie, with real actors and a decent budget. It wasn't going to be a gritty horror movie either – it was going to be a fun crime caper with action, humor and romance. Sam wrote the script with new pals the Coen brothers, and we got a whopping 2.5 million to make it – life was good!

But the production of *Crimewave* was "troubled." I was told I could not be the leading man. Bad weather, long hours and a large crew, earning union wages, sent us from two-and-a-half million to four, and all hell broke loose. In Hollywood, when you go over budget to a certain degree, the filmmakers lose control over their own movie, and that's basically what happened. The film was re-edited, re-titled and "dumped" in theaters in Alaska and Kansas, just to satisfy a sale to Showtime so they could say it had a "theatrical run."

Thinking we had made a charming, zany film that would make a bazillion dollars, we were now in a tough spot. Was this the end of the road for us in a business we had just clawed our way into?

I think Sam had the idea first. "What if Ash didn't die?" he posed inquisitively. "Maybe we tell the next story of his adventures."

Rob was on board, and it seemed as good of an idea as any to save ourselves from artistic doom, so the search for money began. We didn't think it would be a problem, based on the success of the first *Evil Dead*, but because *Crimewave* had laid such an egg, securing the moola became more problematic than we thought. Oddly enough, Coca-Cola was even in the mix for funding at one point through some convoluted subsidiary, but that never came to fruition – probably a good idea.

We were groping in the dark, but in the meantime,

budgets and schedules were being assembled in case we got lucky. Elizabeth Scherberger, an assistant director, helped us with that until we could no longer keep her on payroll. We wished her well, and she was off to North Carolina, where a lot of movies were being made.

Unbeknownst to us, Elizabeth got a job as an assistant director on *Maximum Overdrive* – directed by none other than Stephen King. Apparently, they got to shooting the shit on set and he asked her what she had been up to. Elizabeth explained that she had been prepping *Evil Dead II*, but we couldn't get the money together and had to let her go.

Without missing a beat, Stephen King said, "I'll talk to Dino," meaning Dino De Laurentiis, the larger-than-life producer who had moved his production empire to Wilmington, North Carolina, of all places.

Next thing we knew, we were in Dino's office. He was behind his enormous desk, reviewing the foreign sales of *Evil Dead*. Dino began making movies in Italy and knew the foreign market better than anyone. He looked up through a haze of cigar smoke and slapped his hands together once – whack! "All right! We'll make-a-your movie!"

It was the quickest money deal we had ever been involved in.

The production of *Evil Dead II* was the antithesis of *Crimewave*. We wanted to get this one right – we didn't want to lose control ever again. Planning was better. Time management was better and we didn't spend a penny over the 3.6 million budget.

Over the decades, *Evil Dead II* has landed in a good place within the *Evil Dead* oeuvre and helped coin the phrase "splatstick" – a combination of horror and comedy not seen much before. The movie also sent me west, never to return. I knew I couldn't hide in the protective cocoon of Detroit if I really wanted to be a professional actor. *Evil Dead II* gave me enough ammo to make the move and I have never looked back.

So, thank you, Stephen King. Beyond your enormous contribution to the horror genre for decades, thank you for shepherding us through not just one movie – but *two*. The first *Evil Dead* got me into the business, and the second one saved my professional hide – and for that, I will forever be grateful.

WALK
THIS
WAY

In 2004, when my father died that fall, I did what family members do when a loved one moves on – I went through his stuff. My dad wasn't a hoarder, so he didn't have that much to sort through. He was an avid reader, so there were plenty of books, but a series of spiral binders caught my eye. They were Charlie's "Walking Log," something he updated every day, since he seemed to walk almost every day since the 1970's.

I was astounded to see that Charles Newton Campbell, Kool cigarette smoker for thirty years, had walked 20,000 miles – almost around the entire planet! I knew that my dad took walks, but I didn't know how methodical he had been – for decades – every mile logged in different inks and pencils along with date and brief weather notation. For a guy who was never super-athletic, this was and *still is* impressive.

I recently did a book tour that brought me through the upstate New York area. My grandfather was from Geneseo, New York, a bucolic town outside of Buffalo. Seeing the old family graveyard fueled nostalgia, and I went back to revisit his Wanamaker Diary from 1909. That young man walked to each grade of school, walked to church twice a week and walked to an endless stream of live performances at the local theater.

As a kid, I would often disappear into the woods all day. I walked to middle school and went everywhere else on my bicycle, so in that sense I wasn't much different than my grandfather getting around.

I've been stuck on location for decades. Often, especially in the early days, I didn't get a rental car as part of my deal and I didn't get to choose where my hotel was located. Often, I would be plunked in a name brand hotel in what I call "cloverleaf hell." What that means is you are dumped in a strange tangle of off-ramps, service roads and massive hotel parking lots. When developers put hotels and bars and restaurants near each other, they aren't responsible for how you would get from one to the other. With the assumed mode being automobile, that's where the infrastructure money goes.

Over the years, I have seen my share of infrastructure foibles. If I were a musician, I would write a song called "Infrastructure Blues." On foot, I have been dead-ended, re-routed and bypassed in every major city in this country — and I'm here to tell you I'm not a fan of American infrastructure.

Cars can get around this country pretty well, but the poor schlub on foot really gets sloppy seconds. I'm not going to name any names (Atlanta), but there are some cities that – like my hometown of Detroit – that are criminally under-*infrastructured*. If that wasn't a word before, it is now.

A gallery of infrastructure fails.

I begrudgingly acknowledge that there is better attention to sidewalks and bike lanes in new construction, and some cities seemed to figure it out from the get-go. I went through Amsterdam on tour a few years ago and got to ride a bicycle, Dutch style. Now, I'm a big complainer, but in this case, the city took every mode of transportation into account and provided dedicated routes for each. Bike lanes didn't randomly end – like in the US – they were a permanent fixture along every road, not just major thoroughfares.

Rail-to-trail bike routes in the US have really gotten my attention. It's a vast network of old rail lines that have been torn up and re-purposed for non-motorized activity. Virtually every state has numerous options available. The awesome thing about these old lines is that they are all on train-friendly inclines and 90% of the time, you won't have a car up your ass.

There are still plenty of nice places to walk. Central Park in Manhattan is a godsend and every time I walk there, I see something new. Paris has the Vincennes and the Boulogne-sur-Mer, two enormous parks on either side of the city, known as the "Lungs of Paris." In crowded, polluted cities, parks are critical for mental and physical well-being. Auckland, New Zealand, has "The Domain" adjacent to the city, and I used it extensively for twenty years – from *Hercules* to *Ash vs. Evil Dead*.

These days, with a better flexibility to plan my travel, I actively seek out hotels that are near walking or bicycle routes. Cities like San Antonio developed their riverfront extensively and more cities are following suit.

One of the main things I always enjoy about walking is it's a great chance to be alone in your thoughts. It's also a great chance to have a long conversation with someone if you need to, because walking can open your mind. Often, an office or hotel room isn't the best atmosphere for an intimate conversation.

Another obvious benefit from walking is seeing things close up and personal, not racing by at seventy-five miles an hour. If you're a fan of architecture, nature or just like stretching your legs, walking is a great idea. I'm not a doctor (I have played one on television), but I do know that walking keeps you limber. As I get into my "sunset" years I have found that the old adage "use it or lose it" is very true. I'm certainly not proposing any type of exhaustive physical regimen, mind you – walking is something that comes naturally and something we should be able to do until we croak.

I have since added two other regimens on top of walking – bicycling and swimming. The bicycle came back into my life while I was making *Burn Notice* in Miami. Florida is a very flat state and it lent itself to riding bikes. Bicycles were adopted on the set of *Burn Notice*, and soon every cast member was riding one.

The thing I enjoyed was seeing how much fun people had riding an old-fashioned bicycle again, sometimes after decades. Even the *Burn Notice* bosses partook. "Oh my God!" Executive Producer Alfredo Barrios shouted as he hauled ass on the local bike path. "I feel like a kid again! I never want to stop!"

This happened over and over again as guest cast members, writers and directors passed through Coral Gables.

Bicycling is an activity that doesn't require clip-in shoes, forty-seven gears or spandex (but I do recommend a helmet). Riding a bike can be done well into your advanced years and these days can be done atop a cushy seat, with front and rear shock absorbers and pneumatic brakes. The beautiful machines available now are not your father's uncomfortable bicycles – you can even get an adult tricycle.

I upped the ante recently by going electric and it might be the smartest thing I have ever done. I live in a mountainous area and riding a traditional bicycle has lost its appeal. My electric bike has the effect of lowering the hills around me and flattening the inclines. Bicycling is also something that hasn't been halted by pandemic restrictions and thank goodness for that – it's independent, rarely gathering and healthy. One positive outcome from this COVID-19 stuff might be that more people will be riding bicycles and that's good news for bicyclists, because it means bikes will get better and cheaper.

The electric beast.

The last regimen I try and do as often as possible is swim. For most people, swimming is a very natural activity, with very low impact and decent resistance. I've used a pool as my gym for fifteen years now and I've done so many routines, I could shoot a workout video – using no equipment. I don't know about you, but I'm not a big fan of activity that requires tons of gear to get exercise.

I re-discovered swimming in Miami also while shooting *Burn Notice*. Those of you that have been there know how relentlessly hot and humid it is, so access to a pool is mandatory. A pool became my best friend when I blew my hamstring fighting a stunt guy. Water took all the weight off of my injured leg and allowed me to slowly re-engage it. I've been a fan ever since.

What I like most about walking, riding a bike or swimming, is that I don't feel like I'm working out. I've had to work out for movie roles in the past and I never enjoyed it. I was never a "gym rat" like some actors. I know myself well enough to know that if it feels like exercise, chances are pretty good that I won't do it.

Another advantage of these pastimes is that they're *cheap*. Walking cost you exactly zero dollars per walk or per mile. With a bicycle, yeah you have to acquire a bike, and electric bikes aren't cheap, but once you lay out the cash, you're really just maintaining after that – and it's not like they need oil changes or gasoline.

Swimming, unless you live out the country, has to be done in a pool, so you need access to a community center or YMCA-type place. The jury is out about re-opening these types of public places, but even small towns have something aquatic available.

If you are fortunate enough to live in the country, rivers are the best to swim in, just for the "revitalization factor." Rivers are traditionally very, very cold – especially the undammed ones, because it means you are essentially swimming in snowmelt.

Obviously, none of this is rocket science and that's the beauty of simple exercises. It doesn't matter what you do as long as you do something every day. We have to move our bodies, or they will atrophy. I know from many years of beating my body up that I'm ready to take it easy. I want to get my exercise — I just don't want to know I'm doing it.

THE LEGEND OF

DON POITEVANT

My property is situated on the top of a hill, south-facing at about 2,200 feet elevation. This only matters because position in southern Oregon is everything. I'm in the foothills of the mighty Siskiyou Mountains, one of the few east/west ranges in the US. As a result, when the sun dips into the southern sky, the northern side is severely light-challenged, creating a completely different ecosystem of shade-tolerant trees, like the Douglas Fir.

Directly "across the street," our side is the "hot" side, favoring vegetation that enjoys a lot of light and heat – like ponderosa pine, madrone and oak. We have some beautiful specimens on the property, but there was a tragic situation playing out near our house. An enormous madrone had died and was slumping over an otherwise healthy oak, pushing it well to the side in an unsustainable position.

As a new property owner and self-appointed "Mountain Man," I heated my small, hobbit home with wood, and I had plenty of it available – all I had to do was cut it up. The offending madrone tree was a likely first candidate for firewood. Aside from being an easy-lighting, hot burning wood, I could also help the ailing oak.

So, we hacked the beast down and sliced it into sizes that we could later divide on my new wood-splitter. This process was fruitful, but mindless. It was a big tree. There was a lot of wood. It was a slog. Eventually, we get down to the very last madrone log. There was an odd crack running through it, but I didn't pay attention as I slammed it down on the splitter. "Last one!" I declared, victoriously.

As I engaged the splitter, the steel wedge slid forward and bit into the wood, but the log didn't split at the impact point – instead, it broke open where the odd crack was and fell into two clean pieces. As I picked them up,

The Split vs. The Crack.

I adjusted my eyes to see what looked like lettering that had been branded into the wood – **on Poite**. The other piece of wood had identical lettering, only reversed, like a mirror image.

Feeling like I was in the beginning of an adventure movie, I studied my find like Indiana Jones. The lettering, carved or burned into the wood, was misshapen – often like you would see in lettering carved into the rocks along the Oregon Trail from pioneer days.

Based on where the wood was cut at each end, there was clearly more to the first word than "on" and there was more to the last word than "Poite" – but what? And how on earth did this lettering wind up directly in the middle of a six-inch thick log? The mysteries had to be solved.

I recruited Ida and we started at the local historical society, but it was a dead end. My local Pioneer Era cemetery keeps records of the interred, but nothing matched. Without a full name, it was hard to zero in on anything, so I put the keepsake on my office shelf and we let it go as a great conversation starter.

Not long after, Ida was attending one of her monthly "Buncom Babes" luncheons. Taking their name from an abandoned mining town in the area, this group's get-to-gethers were always a lively gathering of local women, who eat and gossip and catch up. As conversation rounded the table, Ida brought up our odd find in the madrone. Nobody present could connect the dots, but some of the women present had been in the Rogue Valley for several generations and agreed to ask around.

A couple weeks later, we were having dinner with a group of neighbors and one of the Buncom Babes approached our table.

"Good news, we found your mystery man!" she said with glee.

"Really?" I asked, genuinely intrigued. "You think you figured out the name?"

"Yep," she nodded. "Don Poitevant."

Ida just about dropped her fork. Bingo!

"He used to go hunting back in the Applegate valley with his brothers," our friend explained. "This would be during the depression."

The name filled in the missing gaps nicely. I ran the numbers in my head. Based on her recollections, the carving would be about seventy-five years old. Reviewing the scene of the madrone's death with new eyes, the position of the large tree would have been a perfect vantage point to hunt deer. If you removed my house, an open meadow spreads down a widening draw for several hundred yards

– a perfect clearing for deer to forage and an ideal killing field for hunters.

Obviously, during such outings, before there was even a road back into my area, these guys lived life at a different pace. There was probably plenty of time between deer kills to lazily carve your name into a tree.

I had to think harder about why the lettering was buried so deeply within the log – it wasn't etched on the surface where you would expect. Further study – and earlier attempts to kill madrone trees – revealed that they are an incredibly regenerative species. Cut a madrone down and the stump will have ten new shoots sprouting in six months. The bark is also very interesting, as it sheds occasionally, revealing a completely smooth surface that almost curves around bumps and blemishes, like rubber. My guess is that the tree had seventy-five years for the malleable wood to grow around the carvings and eventually subsume them.

I was glad to have the Don Poitevant mystery solved and I was equally glad for the oak tree, which was now free from its oppressor. The tree has since flourished. It bounced right back up and currently shades the pool I have since added underneath its spreading wings.

THE COOL SIDE OF MY PILLOW

A
LITTLE
EFFORT
GOES
A
LONG
WAY

The Formative Years are called that for a reason. The experiences you have as a child mold you into what you become as an adult. My childhood was a very happy one, but not because there were no problems or setbacks. I had challenges like anybody else but, looking back, I realized that my decisions had a critical impact on the outcome.

Problems scare us and confuse us, but turning our back or running away won't make them suddenly vanish. I have found that staring a problem in the face – *leaning into it* – is the best way to put it behind you.

Growing up in Michigan, delivering newspapers was a great way to make a few extra bucks. For the most part, it was a pleasant, uneventful job – unless it was winter. Winter was a different story. Winter was brutal.

One particular January weekend was a doozy when I was twelve. On Friday, a freezing rain coated the roads with a half-inch of ice. On Saturday, a swirling blizzard dumped eight inches of snow on top of that. Bear in mind, our neighborhood wasn't a flat grid with regular street maintenance, this was a maze of winding, narrow, sometimes hilly dirt roads. We were on our own.

Miraculously, the newspaper distributor managed to get the papers to the top of a steep hill at the edge of the neighborhood, but Mom's trusty station wagon was no match for incline, ice and slush. How was I going to get all those newspapers where they needed to be? The task ahead seemed impossible. But the idea of *not* delivering the papers loomed even larger. After all, the newspaper boy takes his cue from the mailman and the UPS driver – come rain or shine, you *must* deliver.

I put two and two together and figured out a plan. I played hockey on a league at that time and was pretty good at skating. The ice on the roads would provide a familiar surface. We loved to toboggan and had a full-sized wooden beauty in our garage. The solution: lace up my skates, load the newspapers on the back of the toboggan, strap them down and tow the whole rig. It was slow going for sure, but I have never witnessed more sheer gratitude than that day. Every customer, even the surly ones, greeted me with a smile and a handshake for getting the job done. Personally, this was a great example of how a seemingly insurmountable challenge was overcome *and* yielded unexpectedly positive results!

Speaking of hockey, my team was the worst in the Junior League. Eventually, it was time to play the best team. It seemed like a hopeless exercise, since we all knew – even the coach – that we were going to get destroyed. But the coach's advice to us resonates to this day. He told us that just because we were going up against a scary opponent, it didn't mean that we should give up. On the contrary, we had to try even harder.

Our ragged team took his words to heart and played the game of our life. We were sliding into slapshots, checking their star players into the boards and giving them the surprise of their lives. Did we win? Heck no! We got our butts handed to us, but the other team went out of their way to congratulate us.

Ash vs. Jason: The Junior League Years.

After the game, our coach was almost in tears – but not because he was sad or angry. He was overjoyed that we tried so hard to win. To him, it was our best game and we should remember the great feeling of giving it our very best – win or lose. For the rest of the season, we all skated a little taller.

In a twist of fate, I wound up on the best team in Little League baseball. That part was great. The bad part was that I was the worst guy on the team. It was frustrating to watch home runs and great defensive plays being made all around me, but I wasn't a part of them. I struck out at the plate so many times, I'm sure I was approaching a season record.

These are the moments where you have a choice. Do you fold and bemoan your miserable status as "team loser," or do you try and do something about it? I hated the idea of not contributing to the team, so I decided to just plain "get better" at baseball. If I didn't have the natural gifts the sport demanded, I would practice until I figured out some way to hit and catch and throw that stinking ball.

Slowly, almost imperceptibly, I got better – and as I improved, so did my attitude. I figured if I could improve a little bit, maybe I could improve *more* than a little bit. This thinking served me well when our team got into the Little League World Series (the "White Sox" – *us* – vs. the "Pirates" – *them*). The teams were evenly matched. The Pirates won the first game and the White Sox took the second. Game three was important because it could give a mental edge to our team and creative momentum. We needed to win.

With building confidence, I decided to put my fears aside and play the best that I could. During my first at bat I took a fastball in the thigh from their best pitcher, simply because I refused to back away. Don't try that at home, kids – it left a gnarly, circular bruise for weeks. Still, the incident dampened any remaining hesitation and I hit four-for-five that day. During my last at bat, I whacked a grand slam home run that won the game. There was no more glorious feeling than to help the team win – even if it was *really late* in the season (full disclosure, the Pirates battled back and eventually won the championship, but it was a great series).

At the awards banquet, I was humbled to get Most Improved Player. That meant I sucked in the beginning, but it was okay because they were acknowledging my efforts. The icing on the cake was taking home the Best Sportsman trophy as well. The sweet message behind that award meant that I didn't let being a poor player get me down, or negatively impact my team.

These incidents informed me as a young adult. I was only twenty-one when I embarked on the Herculean task with two partners to raise money for a movie in Detroit, Michigan and sell it around the world. The idea still seems crazy to me all these years later, but I had seen how tackling problems usually ended up with a positive outcome, so I was not to be deterred.

The learning curve was enormous. Legal aspects, budgets, insurance, distribution, sales, marketing – it all made our heads spin. We made a series of rookie mistakes along the way, but we never quit – for four years we never let setbacks change our master plan.

Thankfully, over time, my partners and I were able to sell our scary little movie (*Evil Dead*) around the world to great success and it paved my way into the film business where I've stayed ever since.

*With perseverance, my partners
and I could NOT be stopped.*

If there was a moral to this story, it would be this: don't be fooled into thinking that childhood adversities and triumphs have no bearing on your adult life. To the contrary, they *DEFINE* your adult life. The events decades ago proved to me that just because something *seems* impossible, it doesn't mean that it *is*.

TO TELL THE TRUTH

In 2015, I spent five months being harassed by deadites in New Zealand. Not to be confused with *actual* deadites, I was filming *Ash vs Evil Dead* for Starz. One particular storyline had some innocent campers attacked by deadites, and Australian actress Samara Weaving was one of them. Samara did a great job of being tormented by one agony after another and she was really good about all the fake blood – which covered her most of the shoot. Like most professional acting gigs, she did her thing and went her way. As actors, we never know if we will ever see each other again.

Fast forward to 2016, an election year in the US. I was back in New Zealand to film another season of *Ash vs Evil Dead*. Like most people, I was transfixed by one of the most over-the-top political scenarios in my lifetime. I was also taken aback at how nasty things got between parties – and so quickly.

Sitting on set one day – in-between saving the world from evil – I got an eyeful scrolling through the never-ending political chatter on Facebook. A story about a conservative protester who was beaten up at a liberal rally was accompanied by a photo of a disheveled blonde woman with blood pouring down her face. I couldn't help but do a double take at the image.

Holy shit! That's no innocent victim – that's Samara Weaving!

The make-up folks on set got a kick out of the fact that this article had used one of the "blood continuity" photos they had taken in a utility tent.

I try to stay far away from politics on social media, but I had to call this big fat lie out. As you might expect, responses were evenly divided. My favorite comment was someone calling me "a piece of shit." Wait... *I'm* the piece of shit? Not the liar?

The people behind this deception clearly think a couple of things:

1. They feel threatened enough by the political competition to play dirty instead of focusing on the merits of their own candidate.

2. The end justifies the means. This means that a high percentage of self-confessed, God-fearing people are willing to take one of their very own tentpole commandments – the one about bearing false witness – and break it over their disaffected knees.

There's an old saying, "A liar has to have a good memory." Isn't that the truth.

ENTERTAINMENT

Bloodied 'Trump supporter' in hoax photo is 'Ash vs Evil Dead' actress Samara Weaving

Posted June 8, 2016 7:22 pm
Updated June 8, 2016 7:30 pm

INJURIES SUSTAINED FOR THE CRIME OF SUPPORTING TRUMP. THIS IS HOW THE NEW LEFT TREATS WOMEN.

— This is not a Donald Trump supporter who was beaten up at a rally; it's Australian actress Samara Weaving covered in fake blood on the set of the Starz series 'Ash vs. Evil Dead. *Samara Weaving/Instagram*

I had to call B.S. on this one.

~

Telling the truth just makes sense. It's the simplest, most straightforward way to conduct your life. I remember crossing the border from Detroit into Canada with Ted Raimi and my appearance rep, Mike Estes. Our trip involved seeing relatives, renting cars, going to a convention in Toronto, flying out of a different city, etc. It was a business trip, but not all of it. The explanation was a big, convoluted mess.

As we pulled up near the guard booth, the three of us debated about what to tell the agent. The temptation, like my brother Don's approach, is to say as little as possible, or to over-simplify what you're up to.

"Just going to a con," would be one approach.

"Just visiting relatives," would be another.

We decided the best course of action was to tell the full, unvarnished truth – and I was to be the spokesman.

"What brings you to Canada Today?" The Border Guard asked in his usual monotone.

"Business *and* pleasure, sir." I volunteered.

"How so?"

I took a deep breath. "Well, two of us have relatives in Detroit, so we flew in to visit them from Los Angeles, where we live. But, we have business in Toronto, so we thought we would just rent a car and drive from Detroit, then fly home from there."

"What business do you have in Toronto?" the agent asked, still in a monotone.

"Well, two of us are actors and we're going to appear at a convention."

"What kind of convention?"

"Horror, sci-fi and fantasy."

The guard looked at me with a blank stare, then signaled to a staging area off to one side.

"Pull over there, please."

Exchanging glances, we parked and shut off the car. Had our convoluted story caused suspicion? A different border patrol agent sauntered over and asked the same banal question. "What brings you to Canada today?"

I launched into the exact same convoluted story and the agent again stopped me short. "Okay, thanks, enjoy your stay," he said, motioning us on our way.

Authorities love to poke holes in your story, trying to

weed out the bad apples. No doubt one agent shared our story with the other agent, but because there was no wiggle to our truth, we had no problems.

You won't find these shemps in a Canadian gulag.

~

In my early twenties, I was a little hotter under the collar than I am these days. I could get prickly easily – especially when it came to the truth. A woman in the Franklin Junior Players, a group I did a few plays with, was suspected of being a gossip and compulsive liar. Let's call her Barbara. One falsehood that circulated was something about whom I was allegedly seeing. It didn't seem like such a big deal, but I felt like her untruths needed to be exposed. I planted the seed through an actress friend of a scandalous story whereby I was not only dating the person she suspected, but we were *having sex!* I decided to up the ante!

My plot worked well – maybe too well – as the story, courtesy of Barbara, spread within the Junior Players like wildfire. The wrinkle is the twist Barbara added – that the girl I was allegedly seeing was pregnant! Within twenty-four hours, there wasn't a member of the group who could pass me without a sideways glance or subtle wink. I had my smoking gun. The story was fed only to her – she embellished and disseminated it to the entire acting community.

The question now was how to confront Barbara. In reality, I wasn't even seeing anyone, so I innocently invited her on a date. I picked her up and drove to an isolated road I knew from making Super-8 movies. There, instead of heavy petting, I pulled out a dictionary from under my seat and insisted that she define a few choice words I had picked out in advance: *Dishonesty, pettiness, gossip, deceit,* etc.

After her half-hearted answer, I asked, "If you really know what those words mean, why are you so chronically full of shit?"

Barbara didn't have an answer. She was put on the spot and that was the point. The whole affair was very heavy-handed, but now Barbara *knew* that I *knew* she was full of shit.

We drove to Barbara's home in silence. I dropped her off without further incident.

~

I worked with football great Terry Bradshaw on *The Adventures of Brisco County, Jr.* in 1994. He played Colonel March, a military man of questionable integrity. Terry was great in the part, but he was also one of those guys you could sit around and bullshit with for hours, which is basically what we did between shots. I finally asked him something I'd always wanted to ask a professional athlete.

"Hey, Terry, like actors, you guys have 'interview speak,' where you dance around the truth. After a game, didn't you ever want to just come out and say, 'Those guys kicked our ass,' or 'Man, I sucked today.'"

Terry laughed. "I tried that and it blew up in my face."

"What do you mean?"

"I was playing in this game against Green Bay in the middle of a fuckin' blizzard, and I got so cold, I literally couldn't think, so I took myself out of the game. Afterward, everyone wanted to know why I took myself out. I told them it was because I was cold, and nobody in the press believed me! The next day, all the stories were how 'Bradshaw was covering for an elbow injury' or some horse shit, so after that, I decided that telling the truth didn't matter – they won't believe it anyway!"

"I'm going to do a commercial for a walk-in tub one day."
"That's great, Terry."

~

43

The old movie industry joke is, "How can you tell when a producer's lying? When his lips move!" Hollywood is not exactly known for telling the truth. Film studios have had their books inspected for a century because they don't tell filmmakers the truth about profits.

Why is truth not something we seek with all of our hearts? It's a little scary these days, when you can't trust a photo, a video, or even the printed word to be real, or truthful. The likelihood that the media has gone through some form of manipulation by the time it gets to us is very high.

Even a commercial, like the one Ida worked on as a costumer, was telling the "truth" when they said that a certain laundry soap could get chocolate stains out of a dress shirt. Yes, it was true – *that* laundry soap did get *that* very specific brand of ice cream (which had to be shipped across the country) out of *that* specific shirt. That's truth, sure, but you're really dancing around it.

Another commercial Ida worked on was for KFC, and the actress in the scene had to keep a "spit bucket" just out of frame. She was vegan and as soon as they called cut, the actress would lean over and discard her partially-chewed food. So, she doesn't really eat fried chicken. Is that a lie? There are more than a few gray areas here.

The only true reality show, if you really want to play that game, is the security camera footage from 7-Eleven – unedited. The moment you edit one frame, you've entered the world of manipulation. We've all seen the political ads on TV, which are both very well done and insidious. By slowing movements down, even a little bit, a candidate can seem sloth-like, or unintelligent. Words can be truncated, moved, emphasized, taken out of context or printed in bold for emphasis. I know from spending many hours in editing suites that if you scroll through a shot, frame-by-frame, even of a really attractive person, you can find hideous images.

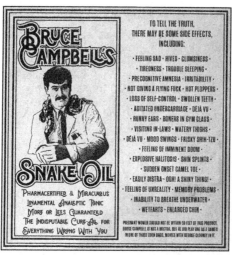

Drugs ads in print have to have a disclaimer about what the drug *really* does to you. The side effect warnings are 7/8 of the ad. Maybe political ads need a disclaimer as well. Candidates would have to explain all the ways that the information presented has been manipulated. That would take way longer than the thirty second ad.

Warning: Most of what the candidate said is exaggerated, underplayed, or factually incorrect.

But, we're all in on the joke, aren't we?

I actually don't have any problem with manipulation

for the sake of entertainment. My second book, *Make Love! The Bruce Campbell Way*, was chock full of fictional anecdotes, counterfeit visual aids, and deepfake photos. The entire idea of the Arts is to get you to believe something that isn't real. Manipulation is necessary to pull off the storytelling.

My problem occurs is when manipulation is used in a truthful context – like electing officials. If you bend the truth in that context, I have a real problem because you're trying to convince people that this candidate is who they say they are and has done what they say they have. How many politicians have beefed up their resumes?

I have flirted with social media manipulation myself, but only in the context of a joke. I've posted a couple of April Fools gags on Twitter and Facebook. One of them,

about me playing the next Dr. Who, went ballistic, and a huge percentage of responders accepted the falsehood, hook, line and sinker. It shows you what a willing public and a clever graphics guy can achieve.

~

I make a living telling lies, but in person I'm a terrible liar. I had an affair during a TV show with a fellow thespian, and I fessed up to my wife before she found out. I had to tell her. It got to the point that I couldn't take the agony of lying any more. The whole idea of an affair is a lie and I didn't want to perpetuate that. Thankfully, my wife Ida is a merciful woman. We worked through that business and put it in the rear-view mirror about twenty years ago, but trust issues echoed for a decade. Lying ruins your credibility and I had to earn it back. I got lucky. My marriage was almost destroyed by a lie, but it might have been saved by telling the truth.

If we lose the ability to tell or perceive the truth, we might as well go back to being tribal marauders. Truth is your *word*. Truth says, "You can trust me." I love feeling like a trustworthy guy. I love trusting other people and I love being trusted.

~

Having just bragged about being a truth-teller, I must reverse myself and admit to one lie – and it was a whopper. My dad Charlie was always a die-hard, *New York Times*-reading liberal. George W. Bush was not one of his favorites presidents. On November 2, 2004, Election Day, my father passed – but not before I told him who won.

"Dad," I said, smiling ear to ear. "Great news – John Kerry won!"

Charlie's eyes focused a bit and he squeezed my hand. "Wow," he whispered.

Charlie drifted off, leaning to one side. I sensed a smile buried in there somewhere.

THE PRINCESS DI FACTOR

You and I killed Princess Diana. That's a bold statement for sure, but there is something to it. Her death came as a result of being harassed by paparazzi. Why did the paparazzi want her picture? Because she was a princess – or because she was a *divorced* princess? Diana was popular when she was married to Charles but nothing like after her royal marriage crumbled. My theory is that she was killed as a result of our fascination with her desire to live a normal life. Intimate or embarrassing photos of celebrities are only worth something if there is a market for them – and we are that market.

In this age of information, it seems like we can find anything we are looking for in almost real time. "Hey, Siri" is a phrase we all know. It's impressive as hell when you think of the technology behind the internet, but I'm left with two questions: *what* are you looking for and *how much* of it do you need?

For starters, I think we're focused on the wrong things. When it comes to quantum physics, or COVID-19, maybe you can never know enough, but when it comes to celebrities, politicians and athletes, it seems like we either don't know anything – or we know way too much.

I have a descending scale of need when it comes to information. If some dude is running for office, a job that has *actual* responsibility, I will want to know a lot about that person – and yeah, medical and tax records too. I would make those mandatory share documents. I also need to know if you're a big, fat liar, so maybe a little digging into your shady business deals would be appropriate.

So why can't we get information on publicly elected officials? We had a sitting president who was an enigma wrapped in a riddle. He was the leader of the free world and we didn't know the guy's health, financial bottom line, or military records. We couldn't get that, but we knew all about Judge Judy's new hairstyle? Do we agree with enough basics in a candidate's platform that we let "the other stuff" slide? I suspect it works the same way on both sides of the aisle.

With an athlete or an actor, I hold those folks to a different standard. If a president is a lush, I want to know that, but if my favorite athlete has a cocaine problem, it should be *their* cocaine problem. Sporting events are entertainment, not détente. These are people in the public eye who can be enormously influential, but they aren't doing a job that involves nuclear codes, so I'm not sure what I really need to know beyond their skill level.

Does it matter if a macho actor is gay? I don't think so – he's an actor for god's sake – and maybe I *don't* want to know that – for my own willing suspension of disbelief. Part of the problem with social media is the amount of sharing – or over-sharing.

Do I need to see inside Ellen's elegant "country retreat?" What do I learn from that, aside from the fact that she has a lot more overhead than me? I think the answer lies in the perception that "celebrities" have something we don't, whether it's money, or fame or a seemingly charmed life.

Honestly, I'm happy to make a decent living as an actor, but I'm glad I never got to a Tom Cruise or Brad Pitt level of fame because their lives are more complicated than you think. These fellows use "burner" cell phones like spies, 24-hour security and enough logistics involved in otherwise mundane tasks to make a guy like me quit the business.

I was in Paris in 1997 when Princess Di was killed in that horrible car crash. I was, in fact, out for a leisurely stroll with my agent at the time, Jeff Goldberg, about a mile from the scene of the crash and close to the time of her death.

Diana's passing haunted me more than other celebrities that have died or been killed. When Versace was gunned down in Florida, I remember commenting about how cold-blooded it was, but were it not for the manhunt and ensuing media feeding frenzy, I'm not sure how much more I would have thought about it.

But Princess Diana was different – her death gave me the willies because of the *way* she died. Maybe it's because, as an actor, I've had cameras jammed in my face by dozens of photographers yelling "Bruce! Bruce over here...hey, Bruce!" I've walked the gauntlet at various functions and even in those controlled environments, the atmosphere of desperation is unnerving.

After Diana's death, "experts" debated the topic, in every form of media, and we tried to make sense of it all. Many folks blamed the photographers, trying to get a dramatic shot, for her death. I'm sure they contributed in their own annoying way, but weren't they just opportunists, chasing a standing offer for photos of celebs? Would callous editors bark out orders for such dangerous, intrusive behavior? Not necessarily, but if the money is good enough, photographers will go to great lengths (as in focal length) to deliver.

The simplistic answer that media outlets present again and again is: "We are merely supplying the demand for stories like this."

Bad news sells.

What's crazy is how the public takes an almost bi-polar glee in building up the famous to unattainable heights and even more so with their inevitable decline. It's all a bit of a shark tank. I tend to think that one thing feeds the other. Actors want to be seen and heard, so they go crazy on social media, but that can – and has – backfired. Social media can become a millstone of obligation for some people in the arts when they become super-influence-y, or it can be their worst nightmare, where the slip of a drunken tongue can sink their freshly-launched ship.

Generally, I try and keep an arm's length approach to the whole thing, avoiding really serious subjects and politics of any kind. I actually get bummed when I find out the political leanings of an actor because in a way, I want to watch them in a role without being influenced by some stance they take in real life. I guess I'm of the "shut up and act" opinion when it comes to celebrities interacting with the real world.

If we spent as much time studying the world around us as we did Kim Kardashian's ass, we might avoid the horrors of war by getting to know our international neighbors better. That's fine in theory, I guess, but some folks in my neck of the rural Oregon woods have no interest in going to another town, let alone another country. They don't even want to *hear* about the outside world. My favorite signs, posted by ranchers in the middle of nowhere, scream about getting us out of United Nations. What would they know about international affairs if they've never left their own county?

When things go awry – and media is taking all kinds of heat these days – we always want to know who is responsible. In this case, the masses can take 100% of the blame. We buy the tabloids, we watch dumbed-down, one-note news feeds, we go to dodgy websites that spew disinformation intentionally without back up or vetting. Why should we be surprised that these things proliferate? If you're tired of the noise, it's not like it's impossible to stop. Just because an outlet is click-baiting you with an inflammatory headline, that doesn't mean it's accurate, or that you even have to open the article. I'm thankful for some headlines, because they convince me not to bother with the rest.

Clicks count. Ratings matter. Success gets copied. Even serial killers spawn "copycat killers." We've learned that flattening a curve takes distance and time. If you want to stop the spread of a media virus the answer is simple: Fewer interactions.

SHANGRI-LA IN UTAH

This is a story of foolishness and near death. I would be the fool and the near death was mine. I worked on a film in Utah in 1988, *Sundown – a Vampire in Retreat* and was exposed, for the first time, to the awesome beauty and solitude of Southern Utah – specifically the Moab area. As a kid in Michigan, I used to lie on my living room floor and pore over maps of Utah and Wyoming, hoping that:

A. Such a place actually existed and

B. One day, I could go there.

Courtesy of the motion picture business, I got a paid trip there. The experience stayed with me – so much so that I returned in 1994 for five days of mountain biking and canyoneering.

I figured the best way to avoid the crush of Southern California traffic was to leave at 2:00 in the morning. As looney as that sounds, it turned out to be a great idea. I was treated to very little traffic (for Los Angeles) and a wondrous sunrise in the desert. I-40 dumped me in Flagstaff, Arizona, about 10:00 in the morning and, after a cat nap under some pine trees, I turned north toward Moab.

Along the way north, I stopped at the Navajo National Monument to look at some cliff dwellings and enjoy some peaceful scenery. If you're ever concerned that the noise levels in our society have reached a terminal level, take a side trip to this magical place. It's overlooking the spectacular Tsegi Canyon system, which hosted cliff-dwelling Anasazi Indians seven hundred years ago.

Go West, old man.

As I approached the look-out spot, I realized that the only sound I could hear was the crunch of gravel under my feet. I don't know about you, but that kind of non-sound doesn't happen to me very often. Across the broad canyon, several vultures went about their business among the sheer canyon walls. It was a rare auditory treat to hear the elegant sound of a bird's wing flaps.

I rolled into Moab about 7:00 that evening and caught the last rays of sunlight from an outdoor café. This type of establishment was new. Back in 1988, Moab didn't even have an ATM and the cappuccino crowd hadn't fully discovered this secret place. Moab has since become the "Mountain Bike Capital of the World." As irksome as that can be, it's better, in my opinion, than what was the town's original activity — a quaint little cottage industry called Uranium mining.

My first full day in Moab was easy. I took a nice bike ride on a wide, dirt mining road on Bureau of Land Management (BLM) administered land just south of Moab. This area is very remote, but not without roads. The Cold War fueled the nuclear craze, which fueled the need for uranium. Moab turned out to have a lot of it and by the 1950's became known as the "Uranium Capital of the World."

When the need for uranium fell off, Moab became just another boom-and-bust mining town, but the desolate area was littered with roads and was soon re-discovered by outdoor enthusiasts. Now known as the "Off-Road Capital of the World," it was very easy to find a random road and follow it for miles through nothing until I found an isolated canyon with big trees and an open, sandy bottom.

My string hammock was up by 11:00 a.m. and I stayed in place all day, writing and listening to the rustle of leaves on the cottonwood trees. Next thing I knew, it was 5:30 p.m. An actor's life!

On day two, attempting some semblance of responsibility, I stopped at the local BLM office in Moab to get a topographical map of the general area. These old mining roads don't exactly come with street signs, so proper navigation with maps or GPS in the boonies is terrifically important – something I had yet to learn. My trusty map showed a trail that had been used by the Mormons and it looked perfect. I'd just bike in, find a canyon and do the same thing as the previous day.

I got to what I *thought* was the right road by 9:45 a.m. There was no marking, but it *seemed* right. I pulled in, off-loaded the bike and took off into the unknown. The road soon began to cut in and out across slickrock – as in no road – but it was rideable and I pressed on.

Stopping for water, I spotted a crude access road across the canyon and decided to double check my map – there was a road, plain as day. *Okay, so I'm not lost.*

This is where happy-go-lucky stories take a turn, and it's why some idiots who cavort into the wilderness every year never come back. Innocent adventures that turn disastrous are often caused by just plain getting lost. Once you're lost, time stretches and you have to survive with enough food and water until you either find your way out or someone rescues you. If you have enough food, but the wrong gear, you'll die of exposure before you starve to death. One way or the other, it's how most amateurs and even some professional explorers "blow it."

I remained undeterred, even as the "road" disintegrated into pure slickrock. Any rational person would have thrown up their hands and turned around, but I can be very headstrong, which is not a top-ten attribute in the outback.

By now, I reasoned, I had gone several miles already and it wasn't like things were dire – the road was just gone.

"Road!? What road!?"

I had been weaving a path that was alternately closer to, then farther from the canyon. Before long, I could no longer ride my bike across the slickrock and was forced to "portage" the thing by walking it at my side as I made my way in and out, up and down a myriad of tributary washes that went toward the canyon.

Finally, in the heat of the moment, I decided to follow one particular wash all the way down to the bottom of the canyon. I had recalled seeing some form of "path" down here earlier. I was convinced that this would be easier. My logic was simple: get to the bottom of the canyon, follow it further inland and come out "right where I want to be." This proved to be a mistake of gargantuan proportions.

Eventually, I worked my way, with bike in tow, down to a source of water – a small, meandering stream. From here, I had a choice. I could go upstream and maybe get back into the slickrock nightmare again – or I could follow the water down its natural course to where I'd find the biggest *main* canyon and *then* follow it inland. Confused? I was too, and the 4.5 hour "Downstream Journey of Tears" began.

Underbrush on either side of the stream was very thick. Usually, I curse any sign of humanity when I'm in the outback, but in this particular instance, I longed for some sign: a coke can with an old pop top, cigarette butts, footprints – anything!

The underbrush got so thick that I had to make another decision – keep up this insanity or do a type of "stream walking." It seemed easy enough. I had my sandals with me. I'll just slip out of my Asolo boots and walk comfortably down the stream, right? Keep reading.

This worked fine for very brief intervals. The Velcro on my sandal straps (Brand Name withheld) was giving out every twenty-five feet or so. But the water seemed too deep every so often, so I tried a sort of in-and-out method of travel: up on the banks for a while until the brush got too thick, then back in the water until it got too deep. Well, the sandal issue became much too tedious, so I switched back to boots and began the *African Queen* portion of this soggy saga. In the classic movie, star Humphrey Bogart has to tow his boat through a festering swamp by hand while being attacked by leeches. In my case, the only thing missing were the leeches.

So – pushing, pulling, half dragging, floating, always cursing, switching sides of the bike, sliding in the muck of the banks, scratching my bare legs on the bike pedals (yep, I was wearing shorts), scraping them on the reeds, shrubs, weeds, above ground and under water – I pressed on.

Then the pebble patrol began. Every twenty minutes, I had to empty the collection of pebbles from my boots – this, by the way, was in addition to the quicksand. It was a maddening series of boot down – FOOMP! Boot up – SUCK! Of course, where there was no quicksand, there were hidden pockets of slippery rocks, or cleverly disguised pools of water up to my chest.

I thought this was a desert!

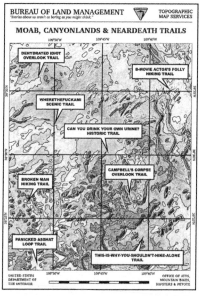

So, like any red-blooded American, I started cursing. I cursed the Mormons, my bike, the topo map, the jets passing above (knowing that they're getting "complementary beverage and lunch service"), my ignorance, fatigue, the basic design of canyons, deep pools, quicksand, pebbles – you name it, it got cursed.

I stopped to purify some of the silt-laden water a couple of times (which ultimately led to the demise of my water purifier) and lunched on a soggy piece of last night's pizza from one of Moab's trendier cafes.

It became clear to me, far too late, that I had to get out. Panic can also contribute to an early death in the backcountry but there was, in fact, a bona fide road on the opposite side of the canyon. Water was getting consistently deeper, and I wasn't getting any younger. From a trip to Moab in 1988, I got a taste of how to climb a sandstone ledge and how to creep up the side of canyon walls. Pretty soon, I'd be a permanent addition to the bottom of the canyon with no way out, except the unthinkable – back the way I came in.

So, I pulled the bike out of this interminable stream and lo and behold – footprints and a hint of a trail! To reconnoiter, I left my pack and the bike down below (who was going to take it?) and headed up to see if there was really an exit.

What lay ahead was a shale incline with a big rock blocking the way over the lip. With much effort, I got up high enough to see the road on the other side. Angels began to sing. After retrieving my gear, I had to carry the bike like a pack and tightrope the over-priced thing past the big ass rock to get out – bike, pack and all. Slickrock never looked so good.

I located the access road, jumped back on my water-logged bike and found the car. I checked the map again, then drove further south to the next dirt road and discovered that I had fallen *one exit* short of the desired Mormon trail. A large historic marker indicated that I was finally on the right road.

Missed it by *that* much.

The world is a noisy place. For most people, this is not news. Almost all day, every day, we are bombarded by some kind of noise, mostly unnatural in origin and not always pleasant. To me, noise is like salt: less is more.

Before the Industrial Age, the most prevalent noises were found in nature, like a rushing river or the crash of an ocean wave. What I love about naturally-derived sound is the variety offered. Oceans aren't always foreground and thunderous – they're also still, almost lapping at times. Rivers don't always rage. Who doesn't love the simple sound of a brook, flowing gently over rocks? Suburbanites spend lots of money trying to replicate the same thing in their back yard.

Wind can be a relentless wall of noise that threatened to drive the early settlers mad, but it also provides my favorite sound of all when it blows gently through a pine tree. That soft envelopment shaves the rough edges off my soul – yet it's so delicate, even the lowly cricket can drown it out.

Nighttime crickets provide a very pleasant ambience – but it's a fleeting sound that tends to be more in rural areas. The funny thing about crickets is that they aren't a constant sound like you hear in the movies. They tend to pulse – from just a few to the whole choir – and they die down not long after midnight.

As civilization took hold, sounds of the barnyard emerged – the bray of a donkey or the cluck of chickens. When heavy industry licked in, we were introduced to sound on an entirely new level and in different, often monotonous forms. What must the farmer have thought about the Model-T Ford approaching with the sonic me-lee of its combustible engine? Compared to the familiar *click-clack* of his horse drawn carriage, it must have been a terrifying first encounter for some.

As the concept of "the factory" took hold, ears now had to get used to the hiss of steam engines, coal-fired behemoths that activated turbos, dynamos, pistons and pulverizers. Blast furnaces and stamping plants seemed aptly named.

As cities grew, a new sound became chronic – traffic noise. This modern addition to life's soundtrack is without end – so prevalent, we tune it out, like modern white noise.

There's an airport in every mid-to-large-sized city, and the roar of jets maneuvering has become imprinted in our DNA. If you live near Colorado Springs, Colorado, you'd better get used to "the sound of Freedom." With multiple air bases and an air force academy nearby, there are few peaceful skies.

The search for a quiet spot (1/4).

~

I spent a decade in Los Angeles and my noise takeaways from that city were helicopters, leaf blowers and blaring music. TV stations all had "trafficopters" (police had their own fleet to chase criminals), so when a chase caused an accident or a traffic backup, the news choppers took off. LA air space was busy and noisy.

Leaf blowers are easy to hate. In Los Angeles, you could set your watch for when the two-stroke demons would begin to drone in stereo. It wasn't just one day out of the week and they'd be gone – in order to "blow" every suburban house, they have to be out there every day of the week.

The third of the Los Angeles sound trifectas was music that seemed to emanate from every pore of the city.

Restaurants and shops would not only blast loud music on the inside, but then they added speakers on the outside, as if to say, "Hey, the party is in here!"

I also got a musical taste lesson any time I drove around Los Angeles. Pull up to a stop light and you'd get a discordant symphony of rap, country and pop – all at way above manufacturer-recommended volumes. Is it a self-fulfilling prophecy that if you listen to music too loud, you lose your hearing – so you have to listen to it even louder? I appreciate that you want to share your intensely loud, distorted music with me, but could you please just shut the fuck up and drive?

I often wondered why someone would crank the shit out of their radio, knowing full well how annoying it is. There is a certain "fuck you" attitude involved, but I think there's more to it. Cities are terminally noisy places. I'm guessing some dudes (and it's mostly dudes) figure, "What's the problem? Nobody can hear me." I honestly

The search for a quiet spot (2/4).

think it's the same with noisy people who live out in the country. They might live a half mile away from the nearest neighbor, which *feels* far, but the incessant report of target practice in their back meadow carries a lot further.

The sound of good old-fashioned radio can be equally jolting, as it emanates from the always open window with musical stings, sounds effects, screaming pitchmen and barking blowhards.

~

Technology has helped in some ways and it will always play a part in how loud we are as a species. Remember boomboxes, blaring from some dude's shoulder, the noise winding its way down the street? Thankfully, there was a one-word solution for boomboxes: headphones. What a "Top Ten" great invention.

Of course, now with all the gold-plated, noise-cancelling, Bluetooth headphones, nobody can hear the actual world around them anymore. Try and ride a bike past a clueless jogger who is in another audible world. A bicycle bell is no match for AirPods.

I will always be grateful for texting. Sure, it causes horrible car crashes and bone spurs in your neck, but the invention of texting also stopped Jerky McJerkface from talking so much on his cellphone in restaurants and bars. Now, instead of talking about nothing at full volume, he can text about nothing in silence.

Cities get plenty of deservedly bad press for being noisy, but suburbs don't get off the hook, sound-wise – not by a long shot. "Sleepy suburbs" my ass. There were a lot of trees in my neighborhood outside of Detroit, so chainsaws were pretty much a standard sound, particularly on weekends, and I know from personal experience that chainsaws aren't pleasant on the ears.

I save a special place in hell for dog owners who let their obnoxious animals bark, unchecked all day long. Dog barking noise wasn't an issue when I was a kid, because in my neighborhood, dogs were mostly free-range and weren't chained up all day. Dog barking, in my experience, has greatly increased. Part of the problem is owners abandoning their dogs while they work all day. Another "pet" peeve of mine is breeding. These days, homeowners who want dogs for security can readily find a dog that is specifically bred to bark! Gadzooks!

~

Over time and experience, I learned that sound was relative. Back in the '90s, I worked a lot in Auckland, New Zealand, which was not a huge city. I was looking forward to getting away from noisy Los Angeles for a while and enjoy a quieter place to work – but Auckland did not provide that.

While acting in and directing *Hercules* episodes, I thought it would be fun to grab an apartment in downtown Auckland and do "the city thing." In my regular life, I only inhabit cities for work purposes. Who knew that Auckland had such a great recycling program, and who knew that they collected so many beer bottles, and who knew that they were all emptied, en masse, at four o'clock in the morning, directly in the alley behind my apartment?

There was also a large university clock bell that rang out the hour of the day – every hour. At first, it was old-school and charming. However, if I spent extended periods of time in the apartment, it became a sonic water torture.

Aucklanders also are capable of consuming large amounts of alcoholic beverages. They have been known to pub crawl in groups and demonstrate their finest singing abilities after the bars close – the din of their strained voices ricocheting off the downtown buildings. *Danny Boy* will always remain a personal favorite.

~

I moved to the country in Oregon for the peace and quiet. I did get that for the most part in rural Oregon, but sound is oddly amplified in quiet places, and if you live on a hill, all the noise from the valley will come up to say hello.

You've read about my love of dogs barking. In rural Oregon, people don't run out and get a mixed mutt for companionship – they get them for protection. Country life isn't particularly dangerous, but people around me are protecting anything from a marijuana crop to exotic sheep. One of the prized breeds to do just that sort of protecting is the Great Pyrenees, who bark excitedly at ghosts all night long.

The country is also mechanized. Folks in the hinterlands like their ATVs and dirt bikes. It almost doesn't matter how far back you go, some yahoo in a motorized vehicle got there first. Aside from tearing the hell out of the back-country, these vehicles are noisy and prevalent. Ironically, manufacturers could muffle the sound, but then you'd be removing the very thing that riders enjoy – the perceived feeling of power – and who could endure the loss of that?

Personally, I love the *clickety-clack* and distant, mournful whistle of a train rumbling along at night, but freight trains are a different story – they are slow and loud. Your rural farmhouse might be lucky enough to be near a freight line which ships as much stuff at night as during the day. The weight of the freight cars changes the familiar cadence of the train and adds a horrible shearing sound as they plod along interminably.

People in America's outback enjoy their guns – daily. There is a butte nearby on public land, where locals for years have gone to basically "shoot shit up." Living outside a city, one does become accustomed to the distant "pow-pow-pow" of semi-automatic weapons, but the addition of Tannerite was new to me.

Developed in the '90s, it's a binary explosive that can be set off only with a high-powered rifle. Primarily, it's used on targets to let long-range target shooters know if they hit their mark. Used in larger quantities, both sound and danger increase. YouTube footage shows one joker shooting a block of Tannerite that had been placed in an old mini fridge. Needless to say, the noise was prolific and the shrapnel almost killed the bonehead. There have been a few "impressive" Tannerite explosions that lifted me out of my chair.

The search for a quiet spot (3/4).

~

One Sunday morning, pretty close to 7:00 a.m., I heard the most bizarre racket reverberating through our valley – and it was getting louder. I stumbled to the drapes and pulled them back to reveal a contraption only a rich pot grower would own – a powered paraglider, racing up the meadow in front of my house! Fearing a crash and ensuing chaos, I raced up stairs to our main balcony, just in time to see this insane rig buzz directly over my house and disappear to who knows where.

The unfathomable noise and intrusion were so unsettling, I called the local sheriff, something I had not done in twenty years of living in the boonies.

"A guy just buzzed my house in some crazy rig, only maybe a hundred feet off the ground. That's gotta be illegal, right?"

"Not as long as he stays under five hundred feet," the patient deputy explained.

Sheesh!

~

I'm not sure if it's because the world is getting louder, but I'm pretty sure that people are following suit. One of the most wince-inducing scenarios for me is the clueless person, walking down the street, sharing their speakerphone conversation with anyone in a hundred-foot radius. It's the new boombox and it presents a twofold problem. For some reason, maybe because of the cell phone cancer scares, most of these offenders hold the phone about a foot away from their ear, then feel compelled to yell into it. What's worse, the vocals emitting from the other end of the conversation are always tinny and distorted, audio dynamics that send me running.

Perhaps most offensive of all are the insipid conversations being broadcast. These people aren't talking about creating a vaccine that will save the world, they're talking about what kind of extra-cheesy, thick-crust pizza they ate the night before.

~

Maybe we actually like noise. Restauranteurs have been known to install "sound reflective" ceilings, which do the

The search for a quiet spot (4/4).

opposite of absorbing sound – they make the place louder than it actually is, in order to create a sense of excitement. Nobody likes a "dead" restaurant, I guess.

I travel a lot and do appearances at convention centers and it's all noisy, which is why I'm bitching about it. I moved away from Los Angeles to provide contrast in my life – and that included sound, which I wanted *less* of.

I was never the type of person who could leave the TV on in the background all day. The same goes for the radio. I can't handle that wall of noise, even if it's low volume. If I had a dollar for every time I asked a cab driver to not only turn their music down, but OFF – I wouldn't have to write this book!

I got a meaningful dose of silence during my "Shangri-la in Utah" back in 1988 (before the experience took a treacherous turn, that is). What struck me on that journey was the *lack* of noise and the ability to focus on one small, natural source of sound. Whether it was the crunching of gravel or the flapping of a crow's wing, I hadn't heard that level of detail in sound outside of an actual recording studio. The experience stuck with me, and I have been a seeker of solitude ever since.

Quiet helps me get centered – like slowing a car in order to calm down a bum tie rod. Whenever I get tired of listening to my own thoughts, a quiet place helps settle the agitation.

So, try to experience some quiet. It might be harder than you think. Turn off the devices, find a back room, close the door and just sit quietly for at least ten minutes. I'm not a meditation guru, so I wouldn't dare tell you what to contemplate during your silence, but think of it as a gift to yourself – the opportunity to think in peace. Silence provides much needed contrast in your noisy life. Try some. You'll like it.

WHAT ARE YOU ON?

I've always wanted to do an animated short film called *What Are You On?* It would be the story of a day-in-the-life of the average American and what he or she willingly ingests.

My film would start with a schlub — let's call him Brandon — getting out of bed in the morning, feeling like hammered dog shit. Why? We'll get there, but first, in order to take the edge off his hangover, Brandon stumbles to the bathroom to throw back some Alka-Seltzer.

Having just put the internal grease fire out, he reignites it in the kitchen with a cup of strong, black coffee. Bear in mind, any drug ending in INE affects the central nervous system, but this is exactly what Brandon is looking for — a substance to jump start his stalled brain.

Because his stomach feels so acidic, he's going to fight fire with an enormous, greasy breakfast, comprised mostly of fried carbohydrates and processed meats. Mission accomplished!

Time to go to his stressful job, so Brandon lights a cigarette, tosses his thermos of coffee into his Nissan Cube and merges into traffic. Each car on the road has a corresponding symbol floating above their car, representing whatever that driver is "on."

A gleaming can of Red Bull floats above a Volkswagen Jetta as it zigs and zags through traffic. That dude is going for the adrenaline rush of caffeine.

The Jetta cuts in front of a beat-up Toyota truck, which has a nicely rolled joint floating above with a trail of smoke twirling behind. That driver is trying to mellow it all out and usually hangs out in the slower lanes.

A minivan passes the sluggish truck, a yellow pill strapped to its luggage rack. Mom might have some anxiety and needs to shave the rough edges off.

The minivan slows behind a suburban dad's Chrysler 300 – the classic martini glass, high-end gin sloshing out of each side, floating above. Vacation in a bottle.

Brandon gets to his job, jittery from the half thermos of coffee and nicotine from three huffed cigarettes. Now, he's ready to shine at work!

Around 10:30 in the morning, Brandon is going to feel a massive slump coming on. The caffeine will wear off and his blood sugar is going to flatline. What he needs is sugar, so the bear claw Danish in the employee break room fills the bill.

By the time lunch rolls around, Brandon is finally

feeling good enough to join a couple of work associates at the local brewpub for fried food in a basket and a craft beer – maybe two. Brandon's lunch will fill his initial void, but it won't last. By late afternoon, he's going to be dragging, so it's time for more coffee and maybe a painkiller for his lower back.

After dragging his ass back through traffic, Brandon can finally relax at home. Mostly, that will consist of a sedentary evening, watching TV, eating pizza and washing the extra-cheesy crust down with more beer.

Brandon has been having trouble sleeping lately, so before bed, he's going to take some Aleve PM and crash. That's going to work until about 3:00 a.m., when his liver starts to process the alcohol and he'll bolt awake, with a mouth as dry as the Sahara because he hasn't had enough water all day.

Cut to the alarm ringing at 7:00 a.m. Brandon opens his bleary eyes after about five hours of fitful sleep and starts his day all over again.

Rinse. Repeat.

One would think that racing through life with our systems full of stimulants, depressants, euphoriants, anti-psychotics and the worst diet on the planet would be counter-productive to earning a living, raising children, maintaining healthy relationships – let alone driving a car – and yet here we are, most of us "on" something.

This isn't a judgement call. I've had a rocky relationship with booze for years – lots of break ups and getting back together again. I liken hooch to a really crappy girlfriend that you stay with, even though it's obvious to everyone else that you are no good for each other.

In the fantasy, the drink will loosen you up in social situations, embolden you when you need it, and relax you when it's imperative. The reality is: drinking is a depressant and deprives you of your energy and vitality. Over time, it robs your confidence. Alcohol is a thief, morning noon or night.

Aside from that, alcohol is expensive (half of your restaurant bill), bad for our health and very likely to cause embarrassment. I don't know about you but being caught naked in the hallway of a nice hotel, locked out of my room (twice!) is not my idea of proper comportment.

Is the party over or just getting started?

So, it's not like I'm Goody Little Two Shoes wagging a scolding finger, I'm right there with you! I've also ingested a fair number of drugs. I still love weed. I'm a "functional stoner." I'm just really curious why we feel the need to ingest things that alter the way we feel, think and act — from the moment we get up in the morning to the time our heads hit the pillow at night.

In the animal kingdom, you don't see squirrels getting wasted. Deer aren't known for partying. Even wolves only howl occasionally. Why are we so experimental? Do we not feel complete? I'm sure with *Homo sapiens* there is much that can be attributed to "the human condition," whereby we feel the need to throw off our mortal shackles and be free – albeit artificially and temporarily – from those limitations.

I believe in physics. What goes up must come down. It's the same with chemistry – every stimulant or sedative will wear off eventually – and when they do, the effects often outweigh the high achieved. Big coffee drinkers will tell you about the headaches they get if they try and quit. Anyone who has ever had a really bad hangover will recall raising a wobbly fist to the sky the next morning, vowing to never touch another drop. Yeah. Right. Until you feel better.

"Street" drugs are obviously a mixed bag of effects and ramifications. I guess some early anti-drug movies I saw in grade school must have done the trick, because I was too afraid to do "hard" drugs like heroin. I almost took my first Quaalude in junior high school, but when my buddy produced the single pill, it fell into the long grass of my backyard, never to be seen again. That was probably a good thing.

I tried cocaine probably three or four times as a young adult. By the time I stayed awake all night for a second night, I realized that the drug had no soul. People "on coke" talk a lot, but it's all horse shit. Coke was the type of drug that made you feel like the center of the universe. If you bought a bag of weed for a buddy, it would still be there the next day. With coke, if you bought some for a friend, it wouldn't last the night. "We can always get him some more." I'm grateful to have dropped that drug pretty quickly. Finding out later that it was often cut with additives, like baby laxative, further soured me on "blow." It blew all right.

Meth is huge where I live in Southern Oregon. As far as street drugs go, it really is the worst of the worst. I don't know, maybe Fentanyl is worse. When you tick off the ingredients, you start to see the horror behind it all: ammonia hydroxide, Drano, Sudafed, battery acid – all synthetic, all the time.

The freaky things about meth is that it's cheap and the effects last for about eight hours. That's a long high! I'm not sure if I want to be grinding my teeth and walking in circles all day, but it sure is popular.

Apparently, for the first thirty days, things roll right along nicely – long distance truckers find it easier to make round trips, and meth provides the confidence that a lot of disenfranchised folks lack. But, over time, paranoia and psychosis settle in and you're off to the races. Any time I see a sketchy dude, walking along an unlit, rural road in the middle of nowhere, keeping pace like he was late for an appointment, I always have the same reaction: *Meth*.

I live outside of Medford, Oregon, and locally it's

known as "Methford." Billboards along the I-5 corridor in the Rogue Valley warn of the scourge with a series of mugshots of the same woman, deteriorating over a short period of time.

In the first of four shots, the woman looks addled, with wild eyes and hair going in every direction. The second photograph shows the same woman, now with scabs all over her face. Apparently, meth makes you think that something is literally "under your skin" and you have to get to it. The third mugshot reflects the woman's lack of teeth, caused by smoking the toxic drug long enough to wear the enamel off. In that photo, she looked exactly like a pirate. Dead sexy! By the fourth mugshot, the woman's face was beginning to implode upon itself to the point where she didn't even look like the same person – like she was being eaten alive from the inside. Needless to say, I have heartily avoided that particular drug.

Pharmaceuticals are another kettle of fish entirely. Not "street drugs," these are the "good" drugs, made by professional chemists in well-regulated labs. These would never harm us, right?

Oh? Have you read any of the side-effects that come with prescription drugs? The negative effect descriptions run several pages longer than the actual ad! And talk about irony – prescription drugs often cause side effects that are exactly what you are trying to *prevent!*

Imagine the Vaudeville routine. A guy walks into his doctor's office.

"Doc, doc, I got a problem!"

"What's wrong?" asks the doc.

"I'm depressed. I'm having suicidal thoughts."

"No problem! I have an anti-depressant for you that will do the trick!"

"Great!" the guy says. "I'll take it."

"But..." the doctor warns. "There's just **one** downside with this drug..."

"Yeah? What's that?"

"You might have suicidal thoughts..."

What the fuck? Why would I take that drug – even if I was dying?

My takeaway about pharmaceuticals is that they are powerful and harsh on your system. I've had the "drug talk" with my kids, and I cautioned them most about pills, because you have no idea about the contents or the long term health consequences.

My mother, Joanne, was a good example of how prescription pills can get out of hand – without even trying! For eighty-five years, my mother generally avoided the medical system. She was a practicing Christian Scientist, so things like booze, cigarettes, doctors and pills weren't in her line of sight.

After a stroke and a fall, she suddenly found herself on half a dozen medications, all completely foreign to her. One day, in the middle of a lovely chat while visiting her in the physical therapy facility, she pointed to the wall behind me.

"Oh. There's another one," she said, matter-of-fact.

"Another what?"

"Another spider."

I spun around to look at the wall, but there were no spiders. I turned back, horrified. "Mom, you're seeing spiders?"

"All the time."

Holy hell, my mom is wasted on drugs!

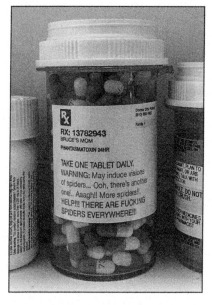

Eventually, I had a sit down with her doctors and we reviewed the meds, one at a time, to see what they did and to make sure she still needed them. We were able to cut her prescriptions in half, but the entire process was unsettling – like watching your wife wash dishes in slow motion.

Normally that wouldn't mean anything, but my wife Ida is a ball of energy and to see her hunched over the kitchen sink, repetitively washing the same plate for five minutes was highly unusual. To clarify, the reason this was happening was because Ida had taken a low dose of Xanax for the first time. To clarify, she did that because I tried to put her in the hospital. To clarify, she almost had a heart attack, because I was trying to make a movie on my property -including the construction of an entire western town – without a financing deal in place.

In this case, Ida was trying to deal with an enormous amount of stress, so her doctor recommended Xanax – for anxiety. Ida isn't a drug or pill person, so she cut the thing in half, just to be safe.

I'm not sure what was going on inside her head, but to my eyes, the drug shaved all the edges off, from top to bottom. Now, there were no lows, but there certainly weren't any highs either. Ida is great at "poker face," but this was a slow-speed pantomime playing out. I dubbed her Underwater Zen Mountain Woman. I also insisted that I get my wife back and that she gets off it immediately.

Easier said than done. You can't just "stop" an anti-depressant. There is a whole protocol of slowly getting it out of your system, so you don't do something stupid – like kill yourself. Eventually, about six weeks later, she was able to wean herself off that single, half dose.

Absurd.

Let's be honest here. Nobody has any idea what happens to your body over time with pharmaceuticals, or how they interact with other medications or alcohol. I'm guessing this unfolding story will have many sad chapters ahead.

But not everyone gets wasted. Some teetotalers, like my mother, live long and productive lives. For many of these folks, their drug of choice isn't caffeine or nicotine, it's organized religion. But can religion be labelled a drug? Can you be "on God?"

Whatever I'm on right now sure is heavenly...

Likening it to a narcotic, religion does "affect mood and behavior" and is used for "non-medical" purposes. People engage in it "habitually" and it can have both "euphoric" and "sleep-inducing" effects (brother, you got that right). Some religious practices are decidedly anti-social and require lots of time, attention and money — always with the goal of attaining "the Rapture." Sounds a lot like being a heroin addict.

If religion is a drug, should it be regulated by the FDA? What would the warning label say?

May cause users to engage in righteous, yet hypocritical behavior.

May encourage death of innocents in the name of said righteousness.

The irony about organized religion is how much "ungodly" deeds are done in the name of all that is good and holy. I guess the thing that keeps me from signing up wholeheartedly with any one group or philosophy is simple: if any of them were right, we wouldn't be suffering through this mess on earth – we'd be flying through the Milky Way with Chuck Mangione's *Feels So Good* playing in the background on an endless loop.

The trick is to not be ignorant about what we're ingesting. We're the gatekeepers. Question what goes in – whether it's from a dealer, doctor or local preacher.

A MOMENT OF ZEN

When I was a kid, I guess you could say I was "on God." I attended Christian Science Sunday school and eventually studied enough to became known as a "class taught" Christian Scientist, which signified a certain level of commitment to the basic tenants of the religion. This essay isn't about all that, but the basic foundation of Christian Science is based on a perfect creator and a perfect creation – and that anything that suggests otherwise is an illusion, drummed up by "mortal mind." Admittedly, living in the material world, it's hard to see perfection sometimes – especially when you're trying to get to the airport during rush-hour in Los Angeles.

I had a business meeting at my agent's office in Los Angeles in the mid-90's. The meeting ran long, which is not a surprise, but by the time I got on the freeway, logistically

I was screwed. According to all material measures – speed of travel, time of day, distance to go, size of the city, with a rental car still to return – there wasn't a chance in hell I was going to make my flight.

I was surrounded on the freeway by a sea of cars and trucks.

Mentally, I was in a funk because all of these stupid people were keeping me from getting home. I could have thrown in the towel and accepted my travel fate, but I decided to challenge the mortal, limited view in front of me. I decided to embrace the concept that if there is a central, benevolent, intelligence looking out for us, then we are *all* in our right place – even lots and lots of us – *right now*. There is certainly an element of mental abandonment when it comes to fully placing your faith in something intangible, but it's a great way to get over yourself for a while.

Mentally, I immediately relaxed. I was going to let "the Universe" – a term I now use a lot – get me on that flight. Traffic on the dreaded 405 freeway never sped up, but it also never stopped. It started to feel like we were all moving in unison to wherever we had to go.

Uncharacteristically, I began to relax and never felt compelled to check my watch during the entire process. I found my exit, dropped off the rental car and caught the shuttle, just as it was pulling away. At the airport, I breezed through security and got to the gate right as the passengers were boarding. I plopped into my seat and the plane door closed – not a hitch, not a glitch.

Looking back, was this a random series of events? Did

I just get lucky in a city where travelers rarely get lucky? The answer, I feel, is that it happened – so *to me* it's real. The second I got away from my own limited sense of self, accepting that there was in fact a universal intelligence running the show – regardless of what things *seem* like – events snapped into place, as if on a cosmic grid. I've had years of spiritual upbringing, but a lot of those teachings hung in an esoteric cloud. It was nice, for once, the see the theory function in the flesh.

I can't say that all my travel since then has been smooth and wonderful, but this experience gave me a new audacity to challenge the accepted norms and unlock the possibilities of something beyond our mortal shell.

We have all heard random stories about UFOs and seen the grainy footage of something in the distance, defying gravity. I had my own close encounter in February 2019.

I've done many interviews over the phone, mostly for PR purposes. These are often low-stress affairs, where I answer a lot of similar questions about the movies or TV shows I have appeared in. Admittedly, I have often multi-tasked during a PR call – checking e-mail on my computer, watching TV with the sound off, or popping some leftovers into the microwave.

In this case, around dusk, I was staring at the beautiful Siskiyou Mountains. The Siskiyous are one of the few mountain ranges that lays east and west, not north and south. So, my view of it in the southern sky is basically a wall of mountains.

As I blabbed about some project, A warbly white light appeared from behind the mountain. There was nothing particularly flashy about it, and it wasn't moving very fast. The trajectory of this craft was pretty much directly toward me. After living on this mountaintop for twenty years, I have become very familiar with the trajectory of commercial jets, as well as their altitude and general speed. Military crafts tend to be higher in elevation than commercial ones, and my little white blob was none of those.

Must be a helicopter, I thought.

Then, directly behind me in the foyer, a buzzing sound caught my ear. I turned to see one of the lights in the entry dim to half for a couple seconds, then back up full. Before I could react, the opposite entry light also dimmed to half for a similar beat, then back up. Sensing that there was a connection between my craft and the odd electrical behavior, I looked back to see that the warbly white light had disappeared from view.

Let's review a few of the odd things at play: First, the craft wasn't out of my sight long enough to disappear, based on its current speed and trajectory and there weren't any obstacles for it to hide behind. I suppose a craft could change speeds that quickly, but none that I have ever witnessed.

Secondly, the behavior of the lights was completely random and irregular. Each inside light is operated by a dimmer switch and is not connected in any way to the light on the opposite side of the foyer – each are on their own circuit. If there was a power outage, based on past experience, the entire house would go out, not selected lights. The same principle would apply to lights dimming. If there was a "brownout," like we have all experienced, all of the lights would have dimmed in unison – not one specific light, followed by another specific light.

My sense of the incident was that the craft exhibited a curious, if not a slight maliciousness in essentially fucking with my lights. It was almost as if someone inside, said, "Oh, what cute incandescent bulbs," and proceeded to "play" with them remotely.

Where I live, when the moon is not dominant in the sky, the stars come out to play. The Milky Way is very plain to the naked eye. When you let your eyes adjust, away from ambient light, you really start to realize that there are an uncountable amount of stars in the sky. If each of them hosted a galaxy of their own, it's crazy to think that there are no other intelligent beings flying around out there. I hope some crazy cool beings are out there. I also hope they help us figure out a way to stop killing each other and remove all the plastic from the oceans.

Sorry, our effects budget ran out of money.

LIGHTS ON THE MOUNTAIN

Not every light on the Siskiyou Mountains is extraterrestrial in origin. Over the years, I've seen flickering headlights plodding along rutted Forest Service roads, which were usually hunters, drug-runners, or occasional "overnighters," partying in the backcountry. This new, bright white light was fixed in place and utilitarian – like the type you would use at a construction site.

I guess we had it coming. Our spectacular view is really a patchwork of logging over the last century, so it's not like pristine wilderness, but there hadn't been any new, destructive cuts in the twenty years that we had been living in Oregon.

I get up early and I will often sit out on my balcony, taking in the pitch-black range – no permanent structures or inhabitants in sight. With a full moon rising above it, the image is hauntingly beautiful.

As a rule, we always have a telescope and binoculars handy for stargazing or wildlife viewing, so I took the lid off my strongest scope and focused on the solitary light. A work operation was, in fact, gearing up. As the sun came up, I could see the full reality – multiple trucks gathered around a landing where men were setting up a large winch – sure signs of a logging operation. To be fair, it's not like it was an illegal operation. A quick call confirmed that it was private property, formerly owned by a pear-packing operation in nearby Medford. Crates to ship the pears had to come from somewhere.

There wasn't anything I could do, so I headed off to New Zealand for the next five months to get doused in fake blood for Season Three of *Ash vs. Evil Dead*.

The men on the mountain were busy during my time away and managed to clear-cut the designated area. The term "clear-cut" applies to the type of logging where every tree is removed during the process. Timber industry folks

bristle at the harsh term and prefer the term "regeneration cut," with "no green tree retention" – great wordsmithing for "we're taking every tree in sight."

I'm only bothered because I'm a tree hugger. I love the term. It's not meant to be flattering, but it really is an apt phrase. I love trees. Hugging them isn't something I've actually done more than a few times, but I can't get enough of trees. I'm not really sure why everyone isn't on board with the fact that trees are essential to life on earth. Aside from fabulous gifts like shade, trees provide oxygen, habitat and slope stability. "The woods" wouldn't be the woods without them.

And yet, we treat trees like they're in our way – which I guess they are, if you think about how many humans are crawling around the earth. I get that trees are a renewable resource, great for making all kinds of things – things we use every day. It is not lost on me that the nasty new clear-cuts in my view are directly related to the toilet paper in my bathroom. What gets me is how oddly the world has approached this whole "land stewardship" thing. Line up ten people in front of the same forest and ask them how they would manage it. Responses would range from "take it all" to "don't touch it."

I don't need a subscription to Sierra Club magazine to tell me that our forests aren't what they used to be. I fly a lot and every time I pass over northern California, Oregon and Washington, I am stunned by the "crazy quilt" of logging practices I see executed on the ground. The patterns are unmistakable because most of the logging is clear-cutting, regardless of location, slope or elevation. It's easy to dislike that approach to land stewardship – it's lazy and it pretty much guarantees an area that it will never be the same.

And yes, I do appreciate the irony that these opinions are from the guy who made a living with a chainsaw mounted to his arm!

The idea of a timber sale is to extract trees and send them to market – but original forests are not made up of just one species. If you rip it all out and plant a singular species back, you now have a plantation, not a forest. My problem with plantations is that if you get a disease that affects, say Douglas Fir, it will wipe the entire plantation out. A diverse forest would still retain some life after an infestation. The timber industry loves to brag about how many trees they have replanted. That's really great, but the trees are re-planted much closer together than Mother Nature intended, so it's really a Roman candle effect when fire arrives, which it will.

So, are the private timber companies doing anything illegal when they clear-cut on their own private land? Most of the time the answer is no. Legally, as a landowner, I could remove every tree from my property. I might catch hell from some neighbors, but my "private property" rights give me that ability.

~

How did our forests get like this? How did *we* get like this? Our ideas are shaped by how we are taught to look at the land. Indigenous people tended to take better care of their surroundings, mainly because they lived *among* the forest, not in the suburbs, separated from it. The forest wasn't just a pretty place to original peoples – it represented survival, so they knew not to screw it up.

The pioneers who landed in what became America, centuries later, were escaping environmental degradation in their own countries. Europe had been logged clean by the time Columbus set sail. Part of the search for a "new world" was for natural resources. Trees were so massive and plentiful, our Founding Fathers were genuinely horrified and cut them down as soon as they could to plant crops.

Let's not forget the religious component of our previous and current land stewardship. The King James version of the Bible lays it all out right in the first Chapter of Genesis:

> *Let them have dominion over the fish of the sea, and over the fowl of the air, and over the cattle, and over all the earth, and over every creeping thing that creepeth upon the earth.*

So, really, it's a matter of how man defines "dominion," which seems wide open to interpretation. There was much more "dominion" after WWII, with a population boom and the mechanization of extraction techniques. Now, better roads could be built in previously inaccessible places, and you could cut way more trees in a day and winch them up to a loader with more powerful engines. Along came helicopters and logging became even easier, if not more expensive.

~

Another reason why our forests are hacked to pieces is due to our overall concept of land "ownership." In the US, land can be owned by individuals, corporations, native tribes, state or federal government agencies.

Look at any map that shows "ownership" and you will see a dizzying patchwork of different colors, representing owners. One crazy example is right where I live. The O & C Act of 1937 sought to straighten out decades of ownership issues relating to a railroad built from San Francisco to Portland in the late 1800s. The idea was that the Federal Government would give a ton of acreage to any railroad builder so they could sell off parcels as the road developed. The government saves money by having someone else pay for the railroad, and the railroad makes their money back by selling off the land adjacent to the railroad. Any time

you have a lot of land in mostly uncharted territory, not much oversight and the potential to make lots of money, greed happens.

In this case, the railroad used middlemen acting as "settlers" to get 160-acre parcels from the Federal Government, then immediately sold them to timber interests, who would cobble the acreage together into large, private tracts. A huge scandal erupted and various acts of legislation ensued. The feds took some land back but agreed to give affected counties a portion of timber sales in lieu of property taxes had the land remained in private hands. Sound complicated? Sure was — and still is.

As a result of all of the divvying up, a huge swath of land — the center part of my state — still suffers from the ill effects of various "owners," each with different steward-ship objectives. A single watershed on these O & C Lands could be managed by the Forest Service, the Boise Cascade Timber Company, the Bureau of Land Management and a Native American Tribe.

My layman's solution is to manage by landscape, not by ownership. Do what's right by the watershed, not the US Government or private corporation. I would log lightly in "snow zones," so that we experience rational thawing. I would also avoid cutting anything near a river or a stream (the Riparian Zone). Surely fisherman and enviros can agree on that. And, if I were emperor of the world, you can take clear-cutting and shove it. I'm for logging, not bad logging.

I would actually get well into our forests and get busy. Rational logging on mostly pre-existing roads can pay for seriously needed restoration projects, like thinning and reforestation. Basically, in my world, every acre logged would pay for an acre to be rehabbed. I would like to see a lot of rural jobs come back, doing *good* work.

~

The West has had some bad forest fires in the last de-cade and increasingly so. Grim-faced locals refer to "Fire

Season" as the fifth season. Fire is fearsome and costly to human life and possessions, but it's part of nature. Forests can't survive without them. Fire is the only thing that will open serotinous pinecones, melting their resin in order to germinate. One of the culprits of an unhealthy forest is fire suppression. In 1933, the Tillamook Burn in Oregon ravaged 350,000 acres of old growth trees on the coastal range. The loss of potential timber revenue was so extreme that measures were put into place to "suppress" fire on all fronts, in all forests. Gone were the days of "letting it burn."

One of the obvious problems with suppression is the elimination of rhythmic "fire cycles." Each area has a traditional cycle when fire does its business to keep areas open and germinate seeds. In my area, our cycle is roughly ten years. So, if you've suppressed fire for eight or nine decades, you've missed the same amount of cycles and forests become vastly overgrown.

A secondary problem of suppression is that it changes the dynamic of the original forest. As forests become denser, "shade tolerant" trees like the Douglas Fir proliferate, choking out the sun-loving Ponderosa Pine. These suppression efforts even impact areas that are still roadless or considered wilderness. Fires were meant to burn, but until the forests are thinned to pre-suppression levels, it will be almost impossible to safely reintroduce it as a natural component.

Greenies, ironically, also have to take their share of the blame for sick forests. While I certainly understand why lawsuits are filed, they have only really succeeded in one thing – stopping action – but "no action" isn't what we need right now. We need action in the woods, just not stupid action. Supposedly, my state has agreed to some kind of interim agreement to limit lawsuits and improve logging techniques. More to come on that.

~

Until opposing factions figure it out, land stewardship begins at home. Whether you have a postage stamp-sized yard, or you're Ted Turner with two million acres, you have a chance to positively impact your little piece of heaven and the world at large. I got a great example of this when I went back to visit my boyhood neighborhood after an extended absence.

The Braes of Bloomfield had (and still does have) heaps of trees. However, one house in particular, high on a hill, hardly had any. As I fished in the pond below, I'd look up and think, *Boy, that's a big yard, but not many trees...*

One day, everything changed. The house sold and the new owners took it upon themselves to plant trees. Not just a few – I'm talking massive quantities. At first, I thought it was pretty cool – the house will have shade, birds will have homes – all that good stuff. But the planting continued. *Okay*, I thought, *enough is enough. All those trees have made it almost impossible to mow the yard*. This sort of thing came to mind because I used to mow lawns as a kid. Extra trees made for a LOT of extra trimming.

Well, it's their property, they can do what they please, I reasoned. I never gave it another thought for about twenty-five years until I swung by the old neighborhood for a look around. Sure, there were a few new homes carved into the woods where I played and the street was now paved, but things pretty much looked the same – except for the house on the hill.

As I drove past, my jaw dropped and I slammed on the brakes. There, at the top of the hill, was a *forest!* For a minute, it flashed through my mind that I had taken a wrong turn at Eastmoor. No, I was a paper boy and I still knew these roads by heart. This was no mistake. Granted, it was a young forest, but it was thick and lush and green. I had never seen a transformation like it in my life. What amazed me most was that the owner had the foresight to think YEARS in advance, not just days or weeks like the rest of us. Somehow, I'm sure, he knew what the results would be.

I was so astounded that I swung my car into the driveway and marched up to the owner's front door. I never met these folks when I was a kid and I assumed that new residents had long since moved in. To my amazement and delight, the man who was responsible for this forest still lived in the house and was happy to chat about it.

Without much prodding, he revealed that he had, in fact, planted over 1,000 trees. Count the zeroes, folks – and bear in mind that this wasn't on a large patch of land, this man owned MAYBE two acres. Needless to say, I shook his feeble hand and told him I thought he had done a grand thing.

As I drove away, I couldn't get the idea out of my head. One person had transformed the land back into something it once was. The whole suburban Detroit area was, without a doubt, thick woods 150 years ago. It had since been cleared for farming and was later carved up into parcels to plant the most prolific crop of all – suburban homes.

As a kid, I saw how dirt roads got paved over and favorite play areas became strip malls or parking lots. You get used to it. We all do. As participants of this advanced age, we take these things for granted – it's all in the name of progress. It was nice, for once, to see the hands of time turned back – just a little bit.

So, go to your local nursery and grab yourself a sapling. Take it home, clear away the rusting car parts in your back yard and plant that sucker. If you feel industrious, plant more than one. If you want to be a hero, plant a thousand!

EVERYTHING I EVER
WANTED TO SAY
ABOUT POLITICS

CLOSE ENCOUNTERS OF THE CELEBRITY KIND

Everyone knows someone who knows someone who knows someone famous. Fame is quite relative. A small-town newscaster is still famous, relatively speaking. He or she might not get a second look in a big city, but when they walk into their local drugstore, heads will turn!

By contrast, even the most famous person in the world is still not known by the *entire* world. I'm not sure that's even possible. Personally, I think the concept of being "famous" is a little off-putting because of how relative it all is – and how it can cause unnecessarily uncomfortable social interactions. It is fun to see how fame affects both the famous and those who interact with them.

As a professional actor, I have had the pleasure of meeting numerous actors who would be considered "famous." Interestingly, my encounters with most of them, like the average citizen, are usually very fleeting – like at a Sci-Fi convention green room – but many are memorable.

Early Encounters

Bruce Clark was the first peer of mine to become a celebrity. We used to talk about girls in his garage tree fort before, seemingly out of nowhere, his father was transferred to London. I'm guessing it was automotive-related as his father worked for one of the big three automakers.

I'll never forget turning on my TV one Saturday morning in 1970 and seeing him in a kids show called *Here Come The Double Deckers*. He played a character called Sticks, and he played the drums. My jaw hit the floor. *How the fuck did Bruce Clark get on that show?* While mind-boggling, it also gave me a slightly more normal view of show business, which previously had me convinced me that it was impossible to get in, unless you were Frank Sinatra – and how did he even become Frank Sinatra?

~

Knowing someone who is related to someone famous presents its own dynamic. In eighth grade, a classmate was Landry Sessions, son of a famous local meteorologist Kelly Sessions. Honestly, when I watched her on the air, I could care less about the weather – she was well-known in Detroit for her hourglass figure.

Her son Landry gave a presentation in class – something about being a doctor and honestly, it was not good. But,

The forecast calls for cold, but that weather lady is hot!

since he was Kelly Session's son, I felt obliged to say something. As Landry sat, red-faced – knowing his own failure – I leaned over and offered, "Hey Landry, that was good."

"Fuck you," was his immediate response.

Now it was my turn for a red face. Landry was a big dude who played hockey – not a guy you wanted to piss off.

To his credit, after a few minutes of cooling down, he turned back with, "Hey, Bruce... I'm sorry."

We eventually got along fine, but that dynamic would not have existed if Landry wasn't related to a celebrity. If he was just Landry Sessions, it would have been just another boring presentation, but because he was "someone," the expectations were immediately *higher*. Why, I don't know, but then, when he failed, it became *more* than it should have been. Personally, I felt sorry for Landry, but ultimately, I felt sorrier for Kelly, who was defrauded by her son years later in a money management scheme.

~

Sometimes, you hear about someone being famous for something and you look at them differently, even though you never saw what made them so famous. My dad was a member of a local theater group, and a fellow member was an attractive woman named Sissy Roebuck. Apparently, she had been "the legs" of the Tareyton cigarette ads.

I was just a lad, so I didn't smoke, but I was aware that it was a big brand of cigarette. "I'd rather fight, than switch!" was the slogan, and the models usually sported a fake black eye. I'm not sure if Sissy had any dance experience, but her notoriety gave her carte blanche to choreograph all of the theater's musicals thereafter.

~

From seventh grade through at least high school, 4:00 was time for *The Three Stooges* on Channel 50 in Detroit. That meant after-school tapioca pudding and violent slap-stick – the perfect combination.

My circle of friends – Scott Spiegel, Sam Raimi and Matt Taylor among them – were all huge Stooges fans. So much so, in 1974, we got the balls to call Larry Fine – the frizzy-haired, violin-playing stooge – at The Motion Picture and Television Country Home and Hospital. Founded in 1942, it really was "The Old Actor's Home," like we all used to joke about.

Larry was one of the few remaining Stooges and Matt Taylor, in particular, was keen on talking to him. Step one was to look up the number of the Home, confirm that

Larry was actually there, then try a call. Living in Michigan, we had to calculate the time difference between us and California and get him at a good time – say 11:00 in the morning, which was 2:00 for us. Lastly, we had to sweet talk our way past his nurse, Mrs. Ross, but that wasn't a problem since Larry was happy to chat with us.

Shemping as Larry.

A stroke limited his clarity, but there was no mistaking Larry Fine on the other end. With a gun to my head, I couldn't tell you what we talked about because I was so nervous, but we flattered the hell out of him, which was really just the point. Either way, I thought it was really cool that a bunch of schmoes from Michigan could just pick up the phone, call one of their comedic heroes and say thanks!

Years later, we took it to the next level and actually hired a great character actor who had appeared in a number of the *Stooges* shorts, Emil Sitka. Scott Spiegel had begun a correspondence with Emil, which led to a phone call or two. Emil's stories were always very entertaining. He was still pretty spry since he was actually a young actor doing those shorts, often winding up in older roles.

Sam Raimi's "mainstream" follow up to *Evil Dead* was the extravaganza *Crimewave*, a Coen Brothers-penned vehicle of romance and adventure. Sam needed a comedic actor to play Colonel Rogers, a funny, crusty guy. Emil seemed perfect for the part and we told him so over the phone. He seemed very excited but admitted later that he didn't believe us until a plane ticket actually arrived in his mailbox in Oxnard, California.

"I was dumfounded," he explained to us later.

As we had hoped, Emil was a font of gag ideas and little comedic bits. He didn't have much of a role, but he milked the hell out of it. My only regret was never doing a scene with him.

Emil Sitka: Master of the Triple-Take.

~

I only lasted six months at Western Michigan University, but a distinct pleasure while there was listening to WKMI, out of Kalamazoo, Michigan. One of the reasons was that my cousin's husband, Bill Martin, was an evening DJ.

The days of just lying in your bed and listening to the radio without multitasking still existed in 1976, and I enjoyed his interviews and the music he chose. What impressed me the most was that Bill wasn't a particularly flashy guy, but there he was, a DJ on the radio!

I know that guy!

I remember calling cousin Nancy to share my excitement. "Hey, I heard Bill last night!"

"How was he?" she would ask.

"Great! He was really smooth! Please tell him!"

Bill really did have a nice, reassuring radio voice. When he passed a few years ago, I shared at the reception that Bill made it seem possible to me that you could actually get a job on the radio – that it wasn't impossible. Before that, the idea of "getting into radio" seemed like a never-ending enigma.

Brief Encounters

Charles Napier was one of my favorite character actors. He had a long and wide-ranging career, appearing in multiple Russ Meyer movies (like *Supervixens*), multiple Jonathan Demme movies (Like *Silence of the Lambs*) and decades of television in-between.

We hired Charles to play Ash's crusty S-Mart boss in *Army of Darkness*. Charles gave a very entertaining performance, but the scene was a casualty of the cutting room floor. Thankfully, I had Charles all to myself on set that day and he did not disappoint.

"I first saw you in that weird *Star Trek* episode where you were playing a delusional hippie, singing, "Goin' to Eden, yea, Brother..."

"I wrote that with Harry Dean Stanton, while we were tripping our brains out in the Rainbow Room on the Sunset Strip," Charles said so casually, it was like he was telling a story about a grilled cheese sandwich.

Russ Meyer movies are a guilty pleasure of mine and Charles had done *four* of them.

"What the hell was that like?" I asked, rhetorically.

"As you would expect. Russ hired a bunch of strippers. He shot those movies in the desert so there was no place for them to go."

~

My boss on *The Adventures of Brisco County, Jr.* was Rupert Murdock, the media mogul and owner of 20th Century Fox. The year our show debuted, Fox was in a major push to establish itself as the fourth network and they were devoting massive amounts of money to make it happen.

Part of that effort involved splashy sales events to round up sponsors for the new shows – in this case, at the Palace of Fine arts in San Francisco. For some reason, I got picked up at the nearby hotel and shoved into a waiting limousine with none other than Rupert Murdock. The car had two other folks, so it wasn't a one-on-one situation, but I was seated directly across from him.

Rupert exchanged small talk with the woman next to him, then he turned his attention to me — what seemed like his *full* attention. Bear in mind, I don't flatter myself to think that this executive was particularly captivated by me. I think more than anything, he was curious about my outfit, which was the full cowboy costume from the show — holster, gun and all.

I decided to introduce myself. "Good evening, Mr. Murdock. Bruce Campbell. I'm enjoying working on the show."

Rupert perked up a bit, but there wasn't exactly a lightning bolt of recognition.

Wouldn't he know all about his TV shows? I thought to myself. Maybe he doesn't have to.

"...The western show for Fox," I offered. "*Brisco...*"

"Oh, yes, of course," Rupert responded. "How is it going?"

"Great, I think."

"Do you enjoy it?" he asked, looking more closely at my costume.

"I do, sir. Who wouldn't want to play a cowboy?"

Rupert nodded. "Well, good luck with it."

And with that, our brief conversation was over. I could tell because I was no longer locked into his personal "tractor beam." Some execs are like that — they are all in, attention-wise, then all out.

We spent the rest of the ride in silence, but it wasn't necessarily uncomfortable. Actors and executives don't often socialize as they have very little in common, but we both had a similar goal that night – to keep our jobs – so we had that going for us.

~

I had heard that Arnold Schwarzenegger was a practical joker. You hear things like that all the time, but how would you ever know if it was true or not? My suspicions were confirmed when Arnold squirted Sam Raimi in the face.

I was in the commissary of Dino De Laurentiis' new studio facility in Wilmington, North Carolina, prepping to film *Evil Dead II*. This would have been early 1986, when Arnold was also in town working with Dino on his action flick *Raw Deal*.

I was seated with Sam Raimi and Rob Tapert, my *Evil Dead* cohorts. We were trying to decide if we could use Dino's studios. Eventually – and ironically – *Evil Dead II*, a movie that Dino was financing, couldn't afford to be made at his own studio – so we moved on to a different city to make the movie.

While we crunched numbers at a table in the commissary, Sam felt some water land on his face. He didn't think much of it at first, but then a second stream of water hit – a larger stream and with more force. Sam couldn't ignore this, and he looked up to see grinning, gap-toothed Arnold Schwarzenegger himself, blasting away with a pistol squirt gun.

Sam was stunned – and that's a rare reaction. He didn't even know what to say, but Arnold wasn't stopping by to chat. He let out a hearty laugh and walked past, scoping out a new target.

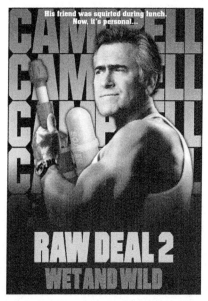

Rob enjoyed the encounter immensely. "Hey, how many guys can say they were shot in the face by Arnold Schwarzenegger?"

I couldn't help but rub it in. "Gee, Sam, why didn't you tell him to stop?"

"Shut up," Sam said, ruefully wiping the water from his face. "I didn't want to have to destroy him."

~

I watched *Gilligan's Island* on TV for a hundred years. The show, perennially in syndication, was one of my viewing staples. *Gilligan's Island* wasn't the greatest show on television, but it was that "peanut butter and jelly sandwich" I could rely on for pleasant, if slightly mindless entertainment. Alan Hale Jr. played "The Skipper," the affable captain of the shipwrecked crew, for three years and enough episodes to sear his image into my developing brain.

Unlike other actors, who chafe at being recognized mostly for one defining – even if iconic – role, Alan Hale Jr. never seemed to mind and appeared often with his ubiquitous Skipper's hat firmly in place.

That was the case when I saw him outside the Sportsman's Lodge after a luncheon in the mid-nineties. As I watched him pose for pictures with numerous fans, I marveled at his ability to instantly adopt a *totally fake* smile that looked at the same time *completely genuine*.

The "fake smile" is a skill I have honed over the years at horror convention photo-ops, but this guy had it down to a science – he would grab the fan's hand, turn to the camera, do "the smile," take the picture, then drop the expression as quickly as he had formed it. It wasn't like he was disingenuous in-between photos – it was just how he did his thing.

Here is my takeaway for creating a useable smile in a photograph – say the word "Okay." As you speak the word, the letter "y" forces your facial muscles into an upward, inverted arch. Practice at home, then try it at your next high school reunion.

Thanks, Skipper!

~

The joke about being an actor in Detroit is that if you ever want to work there, you have to leave. At the end of 1987, I pulled up stakes in Michigan and headed west to be a Hollywood actor. I had been in Los Angeles for only about a month when the phone rang and it was Bob Dyke, a producer/director pal from Detroit.

"Well, looks like we got *Moontrap* financed," Bob said, happily.

"Perfect timing, Bob," I replied, dryly. "I just got out here!"

"Well, get the hell back!"

The film, starring *Star Trek* icon Walter Koenig, was a treat to work on. Mostly, I was delighted that Bob could scrape the money together – something that is always the hardest part of being a filmmaker.

Being the former local boy, I wanted to make sure Walter had a good experience, so I did what any good Midwest boy would do – take him to a Detroit Red Wings hockey game.

By the time we pulled into the Red Wings parking structure, the original *Star Trek* had been off the air for quite a while, but the show had lived on in "syndication heaven" ever since and the movies followed. Even so, the guy at the guard gate didn't notice anything initially, but as he handed me the ticket, he got a closer look at Walter and pointed sharply in recognition.

"Scotty!" he exclaimed, assuredly.

Walter winced and forced a smile. "Nope."

The ticket guy looked again – and guessed again. "Sulu!"

Walter shook his head. "Nope."

125

The ticket guy was getting frustrated at this point. "Well, you ain't Mr. Spock!"

That's when I interjected. I couldn't stand the torment anymore. "It's Chekov! This is Walter Koenig."

The guy shrugged. "Okay. Enjoy the game."

As we looked for parking, I got the feeling that Walter encountered this type of thing before. He was part of an ensemble, led by a strong lead character, so in the minds of fans, he was bound to be tossed into the scrum.

I did get to cheer Walter up a little later while the game was on. A fight broke out and I got to share my one hockey fighting story with him. While playing hockey on the worst team in the league, I got into a scuffle with a guy.

In hockey, to signify that you were ready to fight, you tossed your bulky hockey gloves to the ice. As I did this, my opponent burst into spontaneous laughter.

What's his problem? I thought. That looked pretty bad ass.

That's when I looked down and saw the source of my opponent's scorn: I was wearing my mom's Sunday church gloves underneath to keep my hands warm. Tough hockey players didn't do that, apparently.

This gave Walter something to harass me about for the remainder of the shoot. I complained one day about the cold warehouse we were filming in.

"Maybe you should put on your mom's church gloves," he chided.

"Shut up, Mr. Spock."

~

Bruce: "That's gonna be a cold space walk."
Walter: "Better wear your church gloves."

Networks cranked out a lot of "Made for TV Movies" in the 1990s, and I was in a few of them myself. One such classic was for CBS – *In the Line of Duty: Blaze of Glory* – one of a series of "based on actual cases" police dramas they cranked out. The story of this one centered on a husband and wife who were yuppies by day and bank robbers by night. My co-star was Lori Laughlin, and we had numerous talky, serious scenes throughout the movie. One of our longest pieces involved what is called a "walk and talk," where our characters walk down the street, covering quite a bit of real estate, while we blab – and blab – and blab!

This particular scene was filmed with a telephoto lens in downtown Portland, Oregon. Filming like this can be challenging because it's virtually impossible to "lock down" a city street unless your budget is enormous, so actors had to kind of wing it.

Lori and I were pretty well-seasoned TV actors at this point, so we were ready for anything – or so we thought.

As the camera rolled, the scene played out and we were doing pretty well. But as Lori and I stopped on the sidewalk to face each other dramatically, a person appeared between us, far in the distance. This was not a big deal at first, because everything beyond where we stood was out of focus.

As this person kept walking – not slowly – the assistant directors around the camera started to wave her off. Sometimes, if you catch a bystander's attention, you can get them to get out of your shot before ruining a take. Nothing they did worked, and this woman kept right on walking toward us.

By now, Lori and I had spotted this person, but we sure as hell were not going to stop – we were too deep into the take. So, even with heroic attempts from numerous crew members to derail this determined woman, she just kept walking and eventually cut directly between us, not even breaking stride or suppressing her massive, shit-eating grin.

That's when Lori and I broke character and stared at each other, dumfounded.

"That was fucking Mary Tyler Moore," I said in disbelief.

Lori was equally baffled. "She fucking did that on purpose."

Eventually, we found out that Mary Tyler Moore was in town, shooting a TV movie of her own. Apparently, she decided to randomly have a lark with us on a day off.

Who does she think she is, a comedian?

Full Contact

The Saturn Awards is a geek-friendly awards ceremony, trumpeting sci-Fi, horror and fantasy genres. Although not exactly the Gold Standard of awards, I am continually astounded at the luminaries who show up – like, *real* Hollywood types. This never made any sense to me until big shot producer/director Frank Marshall explained it.

"I've been nominated for half a dozen Oscars," he said, clutching his fresh Saturn award, "but I'll never get one. At the *Saturn* Awards, you win!"

Frank speaks the truth. I don't have an Emmy or an Oscar, but I have three Saturns to my name. Any year a *Star Wars* movie comes out, the entire crew shows up, because they will sweep every category.

I've hosted the Saturns a couple times, given some awards away, and it was always worth doing because I never knew who I was going to run into.

One year, I gave a lifetime award to Janet Leigh and got to imitate Kirk Douglas for her – from a scene in *The Vikings* where Janet is in a ship being held captive and she can't help row.

"My dress is too tight," she protests.

Kirk Douglas reaches up, rips her dress down the back and growls, "Now *row*."

The best part of the encounter wasn't my lame imitation of Kirk Douglas, it was Janet Leigh's reaction – like I was crazy.

My favorite award presentation was to Lee Majors. I

had just worked with him as my dad on *Ash vs Evil Dead* and he was everything you would hope for in a TV icon — no nonsense, professional and funny as shit.

We were lining up a shot on that show and the camera man asked me to hold my shotgun lower in frame because it was blocking Lee's face.

"Ahhh, don't worry about it," I said. "Lee's been on TV for forty years. People know what he looks like."

Without missing a beat, Lee said, "Fifty years."

I was delighted to know that Lee's first role was playing Joan Crawford's husband in the horror movie *Straight Jacket*. Joan chops his head off before the opening credits.

James Cameron was sitting at my Saturn Awards table the year he made *True Lies*. His parents were also in attendance, which was really endearing, as you never heard endearing things about James Cameron as a director. I got the impression he really *was* a geek at heart.

Jim won the top award, which made him very happy and we got to interface briefly afterward. One thing led to another and we got on the subject of "Teatime" – something we had both encountered as directors working within the "English" method of filming, where between four and five thirty, you would stop filming for tea or coffee and assorted pastries or sausage rolls.

It was all very tasty and gave the crew a late afternoon boost, but Jim and I chafed against it as directors. We felt that it was a momentum-killer, so close to the end of the day, and it cost us actual shots.

"I agree one hundred percent," Jim said, with a fiery expression in his eyes. "The first day of shooting *Aliens*, I was supposed to get eleven set-ups. Just as I was making my day, the goddamn tea cart rolls out and kills everything. I only got eight shots."

"Yeah, I had to plan Teatime into my day, like it was a time obligation I couldn't change."

Jim smiled, proudly. "I figured out how to deal with that shit. The second morning of shooting, I went over to the little old tea lady and I said, 'How much?' She looked at me oddly and said, 'How much? The tea is free.' I said, 'No. For *all of this – the whole tea cart – everything.'"

James Cameron solved his problem by literally buying her off the set. "And you know what?" he asked, cracking a satisfied smile. "I made my days after that."

~

You are bound to meet a famous person at some point in your life. My suggestion, aside from *leave them alone*, is to try something a little different. Mark Hamill might not want to pontificate about *Star Wars*. Try a *Corvette Summer* reference. Shatner doesn't want to talk about *Star Trek*. Try chatting him up about *T.J. Hooker*.

I kept that in mind as I entered Chasen's, one of the last of the old-school Hollywood haunts. The occasion was an after-party for the movie *My Fellow Americans*, starring James Garner and Jack Lemmon.

Normally, I wouldn't be caught dead at premieres of movies I'm not in, but this was a chance to meet two of my favorite actors and I was not going to pass that up. The nice thing about these events is that the actors are fair game – it's why they came, to promote, glad-hand and BS with commoners.

Jack Lemmon wasn't hard to find. He was seated with his wife and a few other folks, eating. It wasn't the cleanest entrance – or the best time – but I had my odd-ball ice breaker all set.

"Sorry to interrupt, Mr. Lemmon, but I worked with your son, Chris."

Jack perked up from his dinner. "Oh?"

"Yessir. Summer of 1976 at the Cherry County Playhouse."

Jack drew a blank, but his wife, Alicia, jumped right in.

"The one in northern Michigan? Traverse City?"

"Yes, Ma'am. We both put long hours in as apprentices that summer. He was a really cool guy."

Jack relaxed a bit, knowing that at least his wife knew what I was talking about, but I knew not to wear out my non-welcome. I tossed out a random, "Huge fan," to Jack and disappeared.

One down. One to go.

I spotted James Garner and the geographical layout was not good. He had wedged himself into a corner with two or three dudes in front. That human wall seemed impenetrable.

Just then, a commotion caught my ear. As I turned, an elderly man tripped over a low piano riser and face planted on the floor, snapping his glasses in half and cutting the bridge of his nose.

I hustled over with a couple other guests, and we got him into the kitchen to clean him up and make sure he was all right. I found some tape and jury-rigged his glasses back together. He was shaken up, but mostly appreciative.

"Thank you, young man. You saved my life."

"No problem, sir." I said, fitting his glasses. "What's your name?"

"Jack Garner."

I bolted upright. "Jack Garner? James Garner wouldn't happen to be your brother, would he?"

"Hell yes. Want to meet him?"

All I could muster was an "Uh, yeah…" and Jack already had me by the arm, marching me through the party.

As we got to the same impenetrable wall of people around James Garner, Jack pushed his way right through. "Jim, I want you to meet the young man who saved my life."

I shook James Garner's hand. "Well, I didn't exactly do that, but I did get to play a cowboy on the Warner backlot for a year."

This got Jim's attention.

"I think we were the last Western on Laramie Street,"

I continued. "They tore it down to make Wisteria Lane for *Desperate Housewives.*"

Jim rolled his eyes. "It was a much bigger lot back when I did *Maverick.* The western town ran for blocks and blocks. It was really something."

We exchanged our love of the Western genre and I got to share one of the benefits of being a left-handed shooter.

"What's that?" Jim asked, with a cock of his eyebrow. *Very Rockford Files*, I thought.

"When we line up for a shootout, with my gun on the left side and the other guy's usually on his right, the guns would both be on the same side, and it made for some cool camera angles.

"Huh. Never thought of that," Jim said with a smile. "That would have been handy."

That was plenty of time for me. I thanked Jack for the intro and beat a hasty retreat – two for two!

~

I got a call from my agent, Barry, one random afternoon in the mid-nineties.

"Hey, Mel Brooks wants to call you about a part in his new comedy, *Dracula: Dead and Loving It.*"

"What kind of part?" I asked excitedly. Mel Brooks was an absolute icon of Hollywood comedy and the thought of working with him was hard to comprehend.

"An English king," Barry explained.

"Pass."

"Wait. Why?"

"I can't do an English accent," I explained. "I'm not going to waste fucking Mel Brook's time – even on a phone call."

Reluctantly, Barry conveyed the answer to Mel Brook's office. Twenty minutes later, the phone rang. Mel Brooks was on the other end. He didn't even bother to introduce himself.

"What the hell do you mean you can't do an English accent? Have you seen my movies, Bruce? You think Harvey Corman can do a goddamn English accent? You think that stops him? Get in here and read for me."

When Mel Brooks says that to you, you go in and read – but not before I got ready. I remember cramming with my daughter Rebecca several nights in a row, doing the scene backwards and forwards until I had it "cold."

The audition in Mel's office was intimate and memorable. I was glad I spent so much time on the scene because Mel had me do it fifteen different ways, always bigger and bigger. Mel laughed like an idiot and even escorted me back to my car in the parking lot. There, he backslapped me, wished me well and off I went, beaming.

This part is in the bag! I told myself on the drive home.

Then, as they say in the business: "Cut to tumbleweeds." I didn't hear a peep from the casting office for two weeks – an eternity when you're waiting for a role you really want.

The general rule of thumb in my business is that *no answer*, nine out of ten times, *is your answer.* Casting people only call to share news that you got the role – not that you didn't – because presumably, they would have to make too many phone calls otherwise. It makes sense in a slightly off-putting way.

I didn't care what the protocol was. Mel Brooks had laughed his ass off, and we had a great time. What was the problem? I badgered Barry, and he reluctantly made the call to Mel's office.

When my phone rang, I assumed it would be Mel again, offering congratulations, but it was Barry. "So, I talked to Mel. You didn't get the part."

"Why not?"

"You couldn't do an English accent."

KNOWN IMAGE CREDITS

Cover Photograph by Ida Gearon
Book Composition and Chapter Art by Craig "Kif" Sanborn

The New Deal
    Epic Photo Ops, Celeb Photo Ops and Craig "Kif" Sanborn. Contributing photography by Mike Ditz.

Hail to the King
    Original article by Stephen King appeared in Twilight Zone Magazine. All rights reserved.

Walk This Way
    Bruce Campbell and Ida Gearon.

The Legend of Don Poitevant
    Bruce Campbell and Ida Gearon.

A Little Effort Goes a Long Way
    Charles Campbell and Craig "Kif" Sanborn. Production image(s) courtesy of Renaissance Pictures, Ltd. All rights reserved.

To Tell the Truth
    Ida Gearon and Craig "Kif" Sanborn. Original social media post by Nick Logan. Contributing photography by Mike Ditz. Production image(s) courtesy of Lionsgate. All rights reserved.

The Princess Di Factor
Craig "Kif" Sanborn. Contributing photography by
Mike Ditz and Craig Robinson.

Shangri-La in Utah
Bruce Campbell, Ida Gearon and Craig "Kif" Sanborn.

Shut the Fuck Up!
Bruce Campbell, Ida Gearon, David Jesser, Kurt Rauf
and Craig "Kif" Sanborn.

What Are You On?
Bruce Campbell and Craig "Kif" Sanborn. Contributing
photography by Sergei Kurov. Production image(s)
courtesy of Image Entertainment, Canal Plus and
Universal Pictures. All rights reserved.

A Moment of Zen
Bruce Campbell.

We Are Not Alone
Bruce Campbell and Craig "Kif" Sanborn.

Lights on the Mountain
Bruce Campbell and Craig "Kif" Sanborn.

Everything I Ever Wanted to Say About Politics
Craig "Kif" Sanborn.

Close Encounters: of the Celebrity Kind
Craig "Kif" Sanborn. Contributing photography by
Mike Ditz. Production image(s) courtesy of Columbia
Pictures, De Laurentiis Co., Lionsgate, Magic Lantern
Entertainment and Warner Bros. All rights reserved.

Printed in Great Britain
by Amazon